D0219906

*The Essential
Guide to
Interpersonal
Communication*

The Essential Guide to Interpersonal Communication

Third Edition

Steven McCornack
University of Alabama at Birmingham

Kelly Morrison
University of Alabama at Birmingham

bedford/st.martin's
Macmillan Learning
Boston | New York

FOR BEDFORD/ST. MARTIN'S

Vice President, Editorial, Macmillan Learning Humanities: Edwin Hill
Program Director for Communication: Erika Gutierrez
Program Manager: Allen Cooper
Marketing Manager: Kayti Corfield
Director of Content Development: Jane Knetzger
Assistant Editor: Mary Jane Chen
Assistant Content Project Manager: Emily Brower
Senior Workflow Project Manager: Lisa McDowell
Production Supervisor: Robert Cherry
Media Project Manager: Sarah O'Connor
Editorial Services: Lumina Datamatics, Inc.
Composition: Lumina Datamatics, Inc.
Design Director: Diana Blume
Text Design: Lumina Datamatics, Inc.
Cover Design: John Callahan
Printing and Binding: LSC Communications

Manufactured in the United States of America.

2 1 0 9 8 7
f e d c b a

For information, write: Bedford/St. Martin's, 75 Arlington Street, Boston, MA 02116

ISBN: 978-1-319-06847-9

PREFACE

The Essential Guide to Interpersonal Communication is a versatile supplement for students who need a brief, topical introduction to key concepts in interpersonal communication. It has been designed as a flexible option for use in a variety of speech courses, including introduction to communication classes that do not use a traditional full-size text, "public speaking plus" classes that concentrate on public speaking but also include units on interpersonal communication along with other communication topics, and any class where instructors want to give students a brief but thorough introduction to interpersonal communication.

COVERAGE

The Essential Guide to Interpersonal Communication helps students identify and understand core issues in interpersonal communication quickly and effectively through an approach that combines a solid foundation in communication theory with a clear emphasis on student skill acquisition. Topics include:

- Communication theory (Chapter 1)
- Definition of and functions of interpersonal communication and the elements of successful interpersonal messages (Chapter 1)
- Building blocks of interpersonal communication: self-concept, perception, and emotion (Chapter 2)
- Process of verbal and nonverbal communication and listening skills to apply in personal and professional relationships (Chapter 3)
- Development and maintenance of interpersonal relationships: roles of relationships and individual goals and motivations in relationships, types of relationships, stages of relationships, expectations of relationships, and costs and rewards of relationships (Chapter 4)
- Management of interpersonal conflicts: conditions producing conflict, thinking of conflict as inevitable and healthy, and specific tools for effective conflict management (Chapter 5)

FEATURES

The approach and content of this text are based on the extensive classroom teaching experience of Steven McCornack and Kelly Morrison. Throughout *The Essential Guide*, you will find useful checklists, self-quizzes, and content-review checks that help students understand key concepts and assess their own learning. Compelling features highlight issues vital to interpersonal communicators, such as in the "Put It Together" and "Test This One Yourself" boxes, which help students reflect on different interpersonal situations and move from concept to action.

This booklet is available as a stand-alone text or packaged with *A Speaker's Guidebook, A Pocket Guide to Public Speaking,* and a number of Bedford/St. Martin's communication titles, including the booklet *The Essential Guide to Group Communication.* **For more information** about the Essential Guides, other books of interest, and custom options, visit macmillanlearning.com.

TABLE OF CONTENTS

The Essential Guide to Interpersonal Communication

Interpersonal Basics *1*

Every semester as we team-teach our introduction to interpersonal communication course, we are struck anew by the complexity and richness of relationships, their impact on our overall health, and their importance in our lives. Just think about all the different interconnections that populate your life: acquaintances and roommates, neighbors and lovers, coworkers and classmates, family and friends. And this list only scratches the surface! But across all of these relationships, and the differences that exist between them, one commonality exists: *interpersonal communication*. Interpersonal communication connects us with others, and we use it to create, sustain, and sometimes end our relationships.

We use interpersonal communication all the time, and it comes in myriad forms. On any given day, we may text or tweet, e-mail or post, call people on the phone or chat with them face-to-face—and sometimes we do more than one of these at once. But regardless of how we're communicating, or with whom, one fact inescapably connects all of us: *the communication choices we make determine the personal, interpersonal, and relationship outcomes that follow*. When we competently communicate, we create desirable outcomes, such as personal contentment, positive emotions, and satisfying relationships. When we communicate poorly, negative outcomes may occur, such as discontentment, emotional distress, or relationship dissatisfaction. By studying this *Essential Guide to Interpersonal Communication*, you can acquire knowledge and skills that enhance your competence as an interpersonal communicator. This, in turn, will help you to construct and maintain satisfying relationships and, ultimately, improve your quality of life.

In this chapter, we begin our study of interpersonal communication by exploring the concepts of communication, interpersonal communication, and competence.

By the end of this chapter, you should be able to:

YOUR CHAPTER-OPENING CHECKLIST

✓ Define communication.

✓ Recognize six features defining communication.

✓ Define interpersonal communication.

✓ Differentiate the five truths about interpersonal communication.

✓ State two outcomes arising from the dynamic nature of interpersonal communication.

✓ Define intrapersonal communication.

✓ Define impersonal communication.

✓ Explain three dimensions of interpersonal communication competence.

This book is designed to help you improve your interpersonal communication skills. The starting point for this is an understanding of the concept of communication. We begin by defining communication and considering six important features of our definition.

WHAT IS COMMUNICATION?

The National Communication Association (NCA, 2002), a professional organization representing communication teachers and scholars in the United States, defines **communication** as *the process through which people use messages to generate meanings within and across contexts, cultures, channels, and media.* This definition highlights six features that help us understand communication.

PROCESS

First, communication is a *process*. This means that communication occurs and unfolds over time through a series of interconnected actions between people. For example, when a friend texts you to see if you want to meet her for lunch, you call her back to find out where she wants to eat, and so forth. Because communication is a process, everything you say and do affects what is subsequently said and done. If you tell your friend you're excited to talk with her about a recent trip you took, chances are that "your trip" will be the opening topic of your lunch conversation.

MESSAGE

The second feature of communication is that we use messages to convey meaning. A **message** is the "package" of information that is transported through communication. Messages include everything from spoken words said face-to-face or via Skype or Google Hangouts, to tweets and social media posts. When people exchange a series of messages, whether face-to-face or through electronic devices (smart phones, tablets), the result is called an **interaction** (Watzlawick, Beavin, & Jackson, 1967).

CONTEXT

Third, communication always occurs within a **context**, or situation that helps shape the meaning that is created by the message. We communicate with others in a seemingly endless variety of contexts, including living rooms, classrooms, and workspaces. In each context, a host of factors influence how we communicate, such as how much time we have, how many people are in the vicinity, and whether the setting is personal or professional. Think about it: you probably communicate differently with your romantic partner when you're sitting in class together than when you are relaxing together at the beach. And to accurately understand the meaning of communication, we must carefully consider all of the factors associated with the context, or setting, in which it occurred.

CULTURE

Communication is shaped by our culture, too. **Culture** can be defined as *an established, coherent set of beliefs, attitudes, values, and practices shared by a large group of people* (Keesing, 1974). Culture includes many subsets of how large groups of people intersect, including our nationalities, ethnicities, religions, gender orientations, sexual orientations, physical abilities, and age. We learn our cultural beliefs, attitudes, and values from our interactions with our parents, our families, teachers, religious leaders, peers, and the mass media, and each of these has an enormous impact on our communication (Gudykunst & Kim, 2003). As just one example of this impact, Euro-Americans tend to devote more of their communication to sharing their feelings with relationship partners than do members of other cultural groups, including Asians, Hispanics, and African Americans (Klopf, 2001).

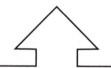

Test This One Yourself

How did you learn about your culture? What was the most memorable message you remember, and who did it come from? How does this message information impact your communication?

CHANNEL

Fifth, we communicate through a variety of *channels*. A **channel** is *the sensory dimension along which communicators transmit information*. Channels can be auditory (sound), visual (sight), tactile (touch), olfactory (scent), or oral (taste). For example, your professor smiles at you and praises you, "You did a fantastic job on your presentation!" (visual and auditory channels). A visually impaired family member "reads" a tactile message you left her, touching the Braille letters with her fingertips (tactile). Your romantic partner surprises you at your home with delicious-smelling takeout, which you then share together (olfactory and oral).

MEDIA

Finally, to transmit information, communicators use a broad range of **media**—tools for exchanging messages. On any given day, we (Kelly and Steve) Skype, text, or e-mail with our sons (all of whom live in different states, from us and each other). We also call, post on social media, write letters, or talk face-to-face with other family members and friends. And we often use multiple media forms simultaneously: for example, we'll sit together in Kelly's office with our laptops, just "hanging out" and chatting while also scrolling through e-mail and checking social media.

Now that we have defined communication, and explored six features characterizing it, let's consider how we can distinguish interpersonal communication from communication.

WHAT IS INTERPERSONAL COMMUNICATION?

Interpersonal communication enables us to construct connections with others. The link that exists between interpersonal communication and relationships is illustrated by our definition: **interpersonal communication** is *a dynamic form of transactional communication between two (or more) people in which the messages exchanged significantly influence their thoughts, emotions, behaviors, and relationships.* This definition underscores five important truths about interpersonal communication.

DYNAMIC

Interpersonal communication differs from other forms of communication—such as a Snapchat, text message, office e-mail, and formal speech—because it is *dynamic,* rather than static, in nature. That is, it flows and changes over time. When you interact with others, your communication and all that influences it, including your perceptions and emotions, fluidly change according to the context and interactions. Two important outcomes arise from this aspect of interpersonal communication. First, no two interactions with the same person will ever be exactly the same. We may effortlessly interact with someone one day and later struggle to understand that same person. Similarly, those we once felt awkward around may become our closest confidants.

Second, no two moments within the *same* interaction will ever be identical. The complex combination of perceptions and emotions that fuel our interpersonal communication choices are constantly changing. For example, you reconnect with an old friend from high school whom you haven't seen in years. After 10 minutes of small talk, you find yourself straining to fill the awkward pauses. You feel uncomfortable and worry that you don't have much in common anymore. These perceptions and emotions will influence the encounter as it occurs as well as how you reflect back on it later.

DYADIC

Second, interpersonal communication is primarily **dyadic**: it involves two people, or a dyad. You chat with your daughter while driving her to school or exchange a series of Facebook messages with a long-distance friend. Of course, some interpersonal communication may involve more than two people. For instance, several family members converse at once while dining together or a group of friends talk while enjoying an evening out. The dyadic nature of interpersonal communication allows us to distinguish it from **intrapersonal communication**, which involves one person talking out loud to oneself or having a mental "conversation" inside one's head.

IMPACTFUL

Third, and perhaps most importantly, interpersonal communication creates *impact*: it changes participants' thoughts, emotions, behavior, and relationships. The impact on relationships is one of the most profound and unique effects created through interpersonal communication. When we interpersonally communicate, we create the potential for meaningful bonds with others.

Interpersonal communication contrasts sharply with **impersonal communication** — *exchanges that have a negligible perceived impact on our thoughts, emotions, behaviors, and relationships.* For example, even though we're married, most of our communication is mundane: things like what groceries need to be purchased, who is going to cook dinner, and what movies we want to watch. Within most close relationships, a fair amount of communication has this impersonal quality. But we can shift to interpersonal at a moment's notice, when needed or wanted. If one of us receives unexpected fantastic news, the other will immediately shift into personal celebration mode, with not just obligatory "congratulations," but personal "You amaze me" messages as well.

TRANSACTIONAL

Fourth, interpersonal communication is transactional, such that both people contribute to creating the meaning in the messages. For example, once you know someone well enough, you may be able to finish his or her sentences. You may create meaning simply by exchanging an understood look or facial expression. This transactional nature of interpersonal communication is enhanced when encounters are face-to-face because creating shared meaning requires both feedback and interplay between partners.

> ## PUT IT TOGETHER
>
> Choose one of the features of communication and consider how it influences the *transactional* nature of interpersonal communication. For example, if you use a channel that is asynchronous, allowing for a delay in responses between the communicators, e.g., e-mail, how does this affect how you jointly determine meaning? How does this impact miscommunication?

IRREVERSIBLE

Finally, although it's not explicitly called out in our definition, interpersonal communication is irreversible. Every time you communicate interpersonally, you and the other person affect your future communication and the quality of your relationship. Consider how you answer your phone. The ring tone prompts you to look at the incoming number. Your identification of the caller influences how you answer, or even whether you do—a warm and enthusiastic "Hi!" or a terse "Yeah?" depending on how you feel about the caller. Your answer in turn influences how the caller responds. And his or her response further affects your next comment.

This interconnectedness of action makes all interpersonal communication irreversible. By posting on Instagram or Twitter, sending a text, leaving a voice-mail message, or expressing a thought out loud during a face-to-face encounter, you set in motion the series of outcomes that follow. Simply put, *once you've said something, you can't take it back.* When it comes to interpersonal communication and relationships, there are no "do-overs" or "get out of jail free" cards. This is why it's important to think carefully before you communicate. Ask yourself, "Is what I'm about to say going to lead to the outcomes I want?" If the answer is no, revise your message accordingly.

Highlighting the impact and irreversibility of interpersonal communication reinforces our central theme with this Guidebook: *the communication choices we make determine the personal, interpersonal, and relationship outcomes that follow.* Through communicating interpersonally with others, you can change your own feelings and thoughts about both yourself and others; alter others' opinions of you; cause heartbreak or happiness; incite hugs or hostility; and create, maintain, or dissolve relationships. This power makes your interpersonal communication choices critically important.

Now that you have a better understanding of the nature of interpersonal communication, let's turn our attention to what it means to be a *competent* interpersonal communicator.

INTERPERSONAL COMMUNICATION COMPETENCE

SELF-QUIZ

Test Your Interpersonal Communication Competence

Read each statement. Place a check mark next to those you agree with.

When I communicate with others, I:

Appropriateness

_____ use the same style of communication regardless of the type of interaction

_____ rarely adapt my communication according to the type of relationship I have with the other person

_____ am not influenced by cultural rules or norms

_____ do not consider how I should modify my message according to situational expectations

Effectiveness

_____ use the same approach to communication regardless of my goals

_____ do not consider the perspective of the other person with whom I am communicating

_____ prioritize my goals over the goals of the other person(s)

_____ seldom think about how my communication affects accomplishing what I want

Ethics

_____ state how I feel even if it bothers the other person(s)

_____ am less than honest if it helps me get what I want

_____ prioritize my feelings over the feelings of the other person(s)

_____ seldom reflect back to consider how my communication affects others

Scoring: Check marks represent competence challenges. The category with the most check marks is the area you need to focus on to become a more competent communicator.

Interpersonal communication competence means consistently communicating in ways that are *appropriate* (your communication follows accepted norms), *effective* (your communication enables you to achieve your goals), and *ethical* (your communication treats people fairly) (Spitzberg & Cupach, 1984; Wiemann, 1977). Although these three characteristics (appropriateness, effectiveness, ethics) are all necessary for competence (and we discuss each in more detail below), no one recipe for competence exists. What's more, although communicating competently will help you achieve more of your interpersonal goals, it will not guarantee that all of your relationship problems will be solved.

Acquiring knowledge of what it means to communicate competently is the first step in developing interpersonal communication competence (Spitzberg, 1997). The second step is learning how to translate this knowledge into **communication skills**: repeatable goal-directed behaviors and behavioral patterns that you routinely practice in your interpersonal encounters and relationships (Spitzberg & Cupach, 2002). Both steps require motivation to improve your communication. If you do not believe your communication needs improvement, or if you believe that competence is unimportant or no more than common sense, your competence will be difficult, if not impossible, to refine. But if you are strongly motivated to improve your interpersonal communication, you can practice and master the knowledge and skills necessary to develop competence.

APPROPRIATENESS

The first dimension of competent interpersonal communication is **appropriateness** — the degree to which your communication matches situational, relational, and cultural expectations regarding how people should communicate. In any interpersonal encounter, norms exist regarding what people should or should not say or do.

While communicating appropriately is a key part of competence, *overemphasizing* appropriateness can backfire. If you focus exclusively on appropriateness and always adapt your communication to what others want, you conform to peer pressure and fears of being perceived negatively by others (Burgoon, 1995). For example, think of a person who always gives in to what others want and never advocates for his or her own goals. Is this individual a competent communicator? How about the friend who always tells people only what they want to hear rather than the truth? As these examples suggest, exclusive attention to appropriateness can hurt both the communicator and those around him or her.

EFFECTIVENESS

The second dimension of competent interpersonal communication is **effectiveness**: the ability to use communication to accomplish your goals. If you can't achieve what you want through how you communicate, you're not a competent communicator. But keep in mind that a single communicative path for achieving goals rarely exists, and sometimes the most competent thing to do is compromise. A critical part of maintaining satisfying close relationships is the willingness to occasionally sacrifice your goals for the sake of your partner, as we have learned throughout the years. For example, suppose Steve wants to catch a band at a local club, but discovers that Kelly has had a bad day and wants him to stay home and watch a Hallmark Channel movie with her. Should Steve say, "I'm sorry you're feeling bad — I'll text you from the club to check on you" and leave? Or should he say, "I can hear this band another time — tonight I'll hang out with you"? The latter approach, which facilitates relationship health and happiness, is obviously more competent.

ETHICS

The final defining dimension of competent interpersonal communication is **ethics**, the set of moral principles that guide our behavior toward others. (Spitzberg & Cupach, 2002). At a minimum, we are ethically obligated to avoid intentionally hurting others through our communication. By this standard, communication that's intended to erode a person's self-esteem, that expresses intolerance or hatred, that intimidates or threatens others' physical well-being, or that expresses violence is unethical and therefore incompetent (Parks, 1994).

To truly be an ethical communicator, however, we must go beyond simply not doing harm. During every interpersonal encounter, we need to strive to treat others with respect and communicate with them honestly, kindly, and positively (Englehardt, 2001).

We all are capable of competence in contexts that demand little of us — situations where the easy choice is to behave appropriately, effectively, and ethically. True competence is developed when we consistently communicate competently across *all* situations that we face, whether they are simple or complex, uncertain or predictable, and pleasant or unpleasant. One of the goals of this guidebook is to provide you with both the knowledge and the skills you need to confidently face challenges to your interpersonal communication competence.

 GAUGE YOUR KNOWLEDGE

Before proceeding to the next chapter, refer back to the chapter-opening checklist to assess your understanding of the chapter concepts.

2   *Interpersonal Foundations*

Now that we have defined communication, distinguished it from interpersonal communication, and reviewed the dimensions of interpersonal communication competence, let's shift our focus to *the foundations that underlie competent interpersonal communication*. In this chapter, we will examine self, perception, and emotions. We will do so because in order to competently communicate with others, we first must understand the factors that shape such communication.

By the end of this chapter, you should be able to:

YOUR CHAPTER-OPENING CHECKLIST

- ✓ Explain the three dimensions that make up "self."
- ✓ Define self-fulfilling prophecies.
- ✓ Describe self-disclosure.
- ✓ Recognize five self-disclosure facts.
- ✓ Define perception.
- ✓ Distinguish between internal and external attributions.
- ✓ Explain the fundamental attribution error.
- ✓ Describe gestalt and algebraic impression formation.
- ✓ List the five key features of emotion.
- ✓ Distinguish emotion from feelings and moods.
- ✓ Recognize primary emotions.
- ✓ Explain the concept of emotional intelligence.

SELF

Although each of us experiences the self as a singular "me," it actually is made up of three distinct yet integrated components that evolve continually over time based on your life experiences: *self-awareness*, *self-concept*, and *self-esteem*. **Self-awareness** is the ability to step outside yourself (so to speak); see yourself as a unique person distinct from your surroundings; and reflect on your thoughts, feelings, and behaviors. Self-awareness is a mirror that prompts you to ask questions like, "Who am I?" and "What defines me?" The answers to these questions are your **self-concept**: your overall perception of who you are. Your self-concept is made up of all the qualities that you believe are self-defining, such as intelligence, attractiveness, sense of humor, generosity, etc. **Self-esteem** is the overall evaluation that you assign to your self-concept, essentially answering the question, "Do I like myself?" Negative evaluations indicate *low self-esteem*, while positive evaluations reflect *high self-esteem*.

Importantly, your self evolves over time, constantly growing and changing. So how does your self connect to interpersonal communication? In two major ways: self-fulfilling prophecies and self-disclosure.

SELF-FULFILLING PROPHECIES

Self-concept and self-esteem often lead us to make **self-fulfilling prophecies**: *predictions about future outcomes that lead us to behave in ways that generate those outcomes.* Some self-fulfilling prophecies set positive events in motion. For example, seeing yourself as a hardworking, conscientious person may lead you to predict that you will succeed at job interviews. This prophecy (in turn) may lead you to communicate in a calm, confident, and professional manner when interviewed, which generates a job offer. In contrast, other self-fulfilling prophecies set negative events in motion. If you view yourself as unattractive and socially inept, predicting negative interactions, you may behave awkwardly when meeting new people, leading them to dislike you and confirming your negative prophecy. As these examples illustrate, a critical component of competent interpersonal communication is envisioning or predicting communication success with confidence. This book will teach you interpersonal skills that will give you this confidence!

PUT IT TOGETHER

Consider how the "impactful" dimension of interpersonal communication from Chapter 1 influences your sense of "self." Recall a conversation that impacted you and examine how it influenced your self-awareness, self-concept, and/or self-esteem.

SELF-DISCLOSURE

Self-disclosure occurs when people share their "inner" selves with others, revealing personal, private information (Wheeless, 1978). Self-disclosure plays a critical role in relationship development, allowing us to create and experience closeness (Reis & Patrick, 1996). Because self-disclosure can evoke vulnerability, responding to a partner's disclosures requires understanding, caring, and support (Reis & Shaver, 1988). When both partners self-disclose and respond appropriately, "intimate" relationships take shape.

Over four decades, and thousands of communication research studies (Tardy & Dindia, 1997), five important facts regarding how people self-disclose have emerged. First, people differ in their comfort levels when self-disclosing: some are naturally transparent; others are more opaque (Jourard, 1964). Second, people in different cultures differ in their self-disclosure. As noted previously in Chapter 1, Euro-Americans tend to disclose more frequently than just about any other cultural group, including Asians, Hispanics, and African Americans (Klopf, 2001). Third, people disclose more quickly, broadly, and deeply when interacting online than face-to-face. During online encounters, people typically can't see the people with whom they are interacting, and so the consequences of such disclosure seem less noticeable (Joinson, 2001). Fourth, self-disclosure appears to promote mental health and relieve stress (Tardy, 2000). Keeping information inside, especially when it is troubling, can escalate stress levels substantially, resulting in immune system breakdown, ulcers, and high blood pressure (Pennebaker, 1997). Finally, little evidence supports the common stereotype (promoted in the mass media) that "men can't disclose their feelings in relationships." In cross-sex romantic involvements, men often disclose at levels equal to or greater than their female partners (Canary, Emmers-Sommer, & Faulkner, 1997). This has led gender and communication scholars to agree that "it is time to stop perpetuating the myth that there are large sex differences in men's and women's self-disclosure" (Dindia & Allen, 1992, p. 118).

TIPS FOR COMPETENT SELF-DISCLOSURE

How can you improve your disclosure skills? By following these tips!

- **Know your self.** Before disclosing, make sure that the aspects of your self that you reveal to others are those that you want to reveal and that you feel certain about.

- **Know your audience.** Whether it's a social media post or an intimate conversation with a friend, think carefully about how others will perceive your disclosure and how it will impact their thoughts and feelings about you.

- **Don't force others to self-disclose.** Although it's perfectly appropriate to let someone know you're available to listen, it's unethical and destructive to force or cajole others into sharing information against their will.

- **Don't presume gender preferences.** Don't fall into the trap of thinking that a woman will disclose freely or that a man is incapable of discussing his feelings.

- **Be sensitive to cultural differences.** As with gender, don't presume disclosure patterns based on ethnicity.

- **Go slowly.** Moving too quickly to a discussion of your deepest fears, self-esteem concerns, and personal values not only increases your sense of vulnerability, but it may also make others uncomfortable enough to avoid you.

Now that we have reviewed the concept of self and defined self-fulfilling prophecies and self-disclosure, we turn our lens outward and explore the processes of perception, attributions, and impression formation.

PERCEPTION

Perception is the *process of selecting, organizing, and interpreting information from our senses.* We rely on perception to make sense of everything and everyone in our environment. Perception begins when we *select* information to focus our attention on. We then *organize* the information into an understandable pattern inside our minds and *interpret* its meaning. Each activity influences the other: our mental organization of information shapes how we interpret it, and our interpretation of information influences how we mentally organize it.

ATTRIBUTIONS

One way we perceptually make sense of our environment and the people within it is to create explanations for our own and others' communication behaviors, known as **attributions**. Attributions answer the "why" questions we constantly ask: "Why did that person look at me that way?" "Why did my best friend post that horrible photo of me?" Attributions take two forms: internal and external. *Internal attributions* presume that a person's communication stemmed from internal causes, such as character or personality. For example, "My professor didn't respond to my e-mail because *she doesn't care about students.*" *External attributions* hold that a person's communication is caused by outside factors unrelated to personal qualities: "My professor didn't respond to my e-mail *because her computer crashed.*"

Our attributions powerfully influence how we respond to others' communication. For example, if you think your housemate woke you up by playing loud music because "she is coping with her devastating romantic breakup," you'll likely communicate very differently toward her than if you attribute her loudness to her being "selfish and inconsiderate."

Given how many encounters we have each day, it's not surprising that we often form invalid attributions. One common mistake is the **fundamental attribution error**, *the tendency to attribute others' behaviors solely to internal causes (the kind of person they are) rather than the social or environmental forces affecting them* (Heider, 1958). For example, communication scholar Alan Sillars and his colleagues found that during conflicts between parents and teens, both parties made internal attributions about each other's messages that contributed to the escalation of the conflict: parents commonly attributed teens' communication to "lack of responsibility," whereas teens attributed parents' communication to "desire to control my life." Such errors make it harder for teens and parents to constructively resolve their conflicts (Sillars, Smith, & Koerner, 2010).

IMPRESSIONS

A second important perceptual process shaping how we interpersonally communicate is how we "size up" other people. The mental pictures we create of who people are and how we feel about them are known as **interpersonal impressions**. Interpersonal impressions vary widely in how they form. Some impressions come quickly into focus while others cohere more slowly, over a series of encounters. Some impressions are intensely positive, others neutral, and still others negative. Despite this variability, interpersonal impressions exert a profound impact on our communication and relationship choices. Two ways we form impressions are by constructing gestalts or using algebraic calculations.

CONSTRUCTING GESTALTS

When we construct a **gestalt**, we create *a general sense of a person that's either positive or negative*, arriving at an overall judgment based on discerning a few traits. The result is an impression of the person as a whole rather than simply a sum of individual parts (Asch, 1946). For example, suppose you strike up a conversation with the person sitting next to you at lunch. The person is funny, friendly, and attractive, and you immediately construct an overall positive impression ("I like this person") rather than spending additional time analyzing each of his or her separate traits.

Gestalts are useful for encounters in which we must render quick judgments about others with only limited information, or exchanges where we can't carefully scrutinize every piece of information we learn. Three examples are brief interviews at job fairs, casual social gatherings such as parties or clubs, and professional conferences. In such settings, you're "mingling" with a large number of people in a short time frame, and so it's useful (and necessary!) to quickly form broad impressions and then store them in memory for future reference.

But gestalts also have significant shortcomings. Once formed, they influence how we interpret subsequent communication of the people and the attributions we make regarding their behavior. For example, visualize someone for whom you've formed a strongly positive gestalt — that is, someone you really, really like. Now imagine that this person discloses a dark secret: he or she cheated on an exam or stole something. Your positive gestalt may lead you to minimize or rationalize the behavior, dismissing it by suggesting that this person "had no choice." The *halo effect* occurs when positive gestalts lead us to positively interpret another's communication and behavior. The counterpart to the halo effect is the *horn effect*, the tendency for negative gestalts to lead us to negatively interpret another's communication and behavior. Visualize someone you loathe. Now imagine that this person discloses the same secret as the individual described above. Although the information in both cases is the same, you likely will attribute this individual's unethical behavior to bad character or lack of values.

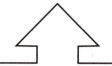

Test This One Yourself

The next time you meet someone for the first time, reflect back on the overall impression you formed. How quickly did you form it? What characteristics led to this impression? How did this impression influence subsequent interactions with this person?

CALCULATING ALGEBRAIC IMPRESSIONS

A second way we form interpersonal impressions is to develop **algebraic impressions**: *carefully evaluating each new thing we learn about a person and using all available information to calculate an overall impression* (Anderson, 1981). We then modify this impression as we learn new information, adding and subtracting different values from each other to compute a final result.

When we form algebraic impressions, we don't place an equal value on every piece of information in the equation. Instead, we weight some pieces of information more heavily than others, depending on the information's *importance* and its *positivity or negativity*. For example, your perception of potential romantic partners' physical attractiveness, intelligence, and personal values likely will carry more weight when calculating your impression than their favorite color or breakfast cereal — unless you view colors and cereals as important.

As this discussion implies, algebraic impressions are more flexible and accurate than gestalts. For encounters in which we have the time and energy to ponder someone's traits and how they add up, algebraic impressions offer us the opportunity to form refined impressions of people. We also can flexibly change them every time we receive new information about people. But since algebraic impressions require a fair amount of mental effort, they aren't as efficient as gestalts. In unexpected encounters or casual conversations, such mental calculations are unnecessary and may even work to our disadvantage, especially if we need to render rapid judgments and act on them.

Now that we have reflected on the foundational aspects of self and perception, let's explore another critical aspect influencing the competence of our interpersonal communication: *emotion*. In this section we will define emotion, distinguish it from feelings and moods, consider primary emotions (see Figure 2.1), and examine the concept of emotional intelligence.

EMOTION

Emotion is *an intense reaction to an event that involves interpreting event meaning, becoming physiologically aroused, labeling the experience as emotional, managing our reaction, and communicating through emotional displays and disclosures* (Gross, Richards, & John, 2006). This definition highlights five key features of emotion. First, emotion is *reactive*, triggered by our perception of events (Cacioppo, Klein, Berntson, & Hatfield, 1993). A friend telling you that her cancer is in remission leads you to experience joy, just as recalling a loved one who has passed away causes you grief. Second, emotion involves *physiological arousal*, in the form of increased heart rate, blood pressure, and adrenaline release. Arousal often is considered *the* defining feature of emotion: the thing that distinguishes it from feelings and moods (which we discuss next). Third, to experience emotion, you must *label* your experience as "an emotion." For example, if you're walking across campus at night and suddenly feel a rush of arousal, you won't experience it as "fear" until your mind thinks, "I'm scared!" Fourth, how we each experience and express our emotions is *constrained by historical, cultural, relational, and situational norms* governing what is and isn't appropriate (Metts & Planalp, 2002). Once we become aware that we're experiencing an emotion, we try to manage that experience and express that emotion in ways we consider acceptable. Finally, when emotion occurs, the choices you make regarding emotion management are reflected outward in your *verbal and nonverbal displays*, in the form of word choices, exclamations or expletives, facial expressions, body posture, and gestures. Other than arousal, many scholars of emotion consider communication of emotion to be the most important defining feature (Mauss, Levenson, McCarter, Wilhelm, & Gross, 2005). The need of human beings to communicate emotion to others is reflected in the fact that people share between 75 and 95 percent of their emotional experiences with at least one other person, usually a spouse, parent, or friend (Frijda, 2005).

FEELINGS AND MOODS

We often talk about emotions, feelings, and moods as if they are the same thing. But they're not. *Feelings are short-term emotional reactions to events that generate only limited arousal*; they typically do not trigger attempts to manage their experience or expression (Berscheid, 2002). We experience dozens, if not hundreds, of feelings daily—most of them lasting only a few seconds or minutes. Common feelings include gratitude, concern, pleasure, relief, and resentment. *Moods are low-intensity states*—such as boredom, contentment, grouchiness, or serenity—*that are not caused by particular events and typically last longer than feelings or emotions* (Parkinson, Totterdell, Briner, & Reynolds, 1996). Positive or negative, moods are the slow-flowing emotional currents in our everyday lives.

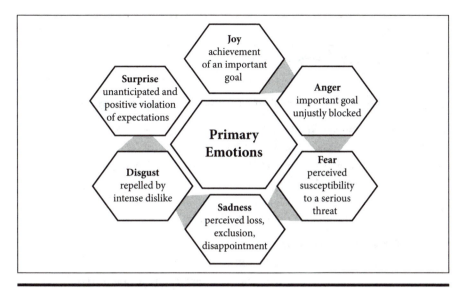

FIGURE 2.1 Primary Emotions

EMOTIONAL INTELLIGENCE

The *ability to interpret emotions accurately and to use this information to manage emotions, communicate them competently, and solve relationship problems* is known as **emotional intelligence (EI)** (Gross & John, 2002). People with high degrees of EI typically possess four skills. First, they acutely perceive and understand their own emotions. They discern variations between emotions; the causes and consequences of emotions; and the differences between feelings, moods, and emotions. Second, they accurately perceive the emotions communicated by others by sensing their behavior cues, such as their facial expressions, vocal tones, and gestures. Third, they constructively manage their own emotions in ways that avoid negative and destructive communication. Finally, they regulate and direct their emotional states toward competent decision making, communication, and relationship problem solving. For instance, when giving an important presentation, rather than allowing anxiety to disrupt their performance, they harness that arousal to act more charismatic and intense.

Given that EI involves understanding emotions coupled with the ability to manage them in ways that optimize interpersonal competence, it is not surprising that people with high EI experience a broad range of positive outcomes. For example, within leadership positions, people with high EI are more likely than people with low EI to garner trust, inspire followers, and be perceived as having integrity (Kotzé & Venter, 2011). High EI individuals are less likely than low EI people to bully people or use violence to get what they want (Mayer, Salovey, & Caruso, 2004). High EI people even find it easier to forgive relational partners who have wronged them (Hodgson & Wertheim, 2007).

SELF-QUIZ

Assessing Your Emotional Intelligence

Read each statement. Place a check mark next to those you agree with.

Considering my emotional experience and communication in my daily life, I:

Perceiving Own Emotions

_____ usually can tell what mood I'm in, when I am in it

_____ easily recognize what emotion I am experiencing, while I am experiencing it

_____ rarely have difficulty identifying my emotional state

_____ do not have trouble identifying my feelings

Perceiving Other's Emotions

_____ am skilled at reading other people's moods

_____ can typically figure out what emotion another person is experiencing

_____ seldom have trouble identifying what other people are feeling

_____ have the ability to accurately read other people's emotional cues

Managing Emotions and Communication

_____ can control my emotions so that they do not interfere with my ability to communicate

_____ am able to manage my negative emotions so that I do not communicate in a destructive manner

_____ have the ability to deal with my feelings so they don't inhibit how I communicate

_____ handle my moods so that I can communicate effectively

Using Emotions to Enhance Competence

_____ know how to channel my emotions in a positive way, such as using anger to fuel intense exercise

_____ am capable of directing my moods to enhance my creativity

_____ have the ability to harness nervous energy in a positive way

_____ can redirect negative emotions in a positive way

Scoring: Count the number of check marks you made. Totals of 0–5 = low EI; 6–11 = moderate EI; 12 and above = high EI.

 GAUGE YOUR KNOWLEDGE

Before proceeding to the next chapter, refer back to the chapter-opening checklist to assess your understanding of the chapter concepts.

Interpersonal Skills **3**

Thus far, we have reviewed some of the foundational concepts of interpersonal communication as well as the primary processes influencing it: self, perception, and emotion. In this chapter, we turn our attention to the actual process of communication, exploring verbal communication, nonverbal communication, and listening.

By the end of this chapter, you should be able to:

YOUR CHAPTER-OPENING CHECKLIST

✓ Define verbal communication.

✓ List two dimensions of competent verbal communication.

✓ Describe four characteristics of cooperative language.

✓ Define nonverbal communication.

✓ Distinguish between four types of nonverbal communication.

✓ List four ways to communicate with body movements.

✓ Recognize four vocal characteristics.

✓ State the four communication distances.

✓ Explain two truths about listening.

✓ Describe the five steps of listening.

✓ Differentiate the three dimensions of active listening.

VERBAL COMMUNICATION

During any given day, we use words to communicate with romantic partners, family members, friends, and coworkers. Our exchanges of spoken or written language with others during interactions, known as **verbal communication**, bridge multiple media: we exchange language through tweets, in Facebook posts, in texts, through e-mail, over the phone, and face-to-face. Depending on whom we are interacting with, we creatively tailor our language, shifting grammar, word choices, and sometimes even the entire language itself — such as sending a Korean text message to one friend and an English text to another.

Competent verbal communication, however, requires that we go beyond simply using language to speak and instead do two things consistently. First, we need to use *cooperative language*. Second, we need to use *"I" and "we" language* and avoid *"you"* language.

COOPERATIVE LANGUAGE

Using **cooperative language** results in messages that people easily can understand because they are informative, honest, relevant, and clear.

Being Informative

Being **informative** means two things: (1) sharing *enough* information, but (2) *not* sharing *too much*. Let's say that a coworker greets you in the hallway with a quick "How's it going?" The situation requires that you provide just a little information in return — "Great! How are you?" The same question asked by a concerned friend during a personal crisis creates very different demands; your friend likely wants a detailed accounting of your thoughts and feelings. So, the first requirement of "being informative" is presenting all of the information that is relevant and appropriate to share, given the situation. The second requirement is that we need to avoid being *too* informative — that is, disclosing information that isn't appropriate or important in a particular situation. A detailed listing of your personal woes ("I was awake all night, my cat is sick . . .") in response to your colleague's quick "How's it going?" query likely would be perceived as inappropriate and somewhat odd.

Being Honest

Honesty is the single most important characteristic of cooperative verbal communication because other people trust that the information we share with them is truthful (Grice, 1989). Honesty means not sharing information that you're uncertain about and not disclosing information that you know is false. Dishonest verbal communication violates standards for ethical behavior and leads others to believe false things (Jacobs, Dawson, & Brashers, 1996). For example, if you assure your romantic partner that your feelings toward him or her haven't changed when in fact they have, you give your partner false hope about your future and allow your partner to continue investing in a doomed relationship.

Being Relevant

Relevance means making your conversational contributions responsive to what others have said. When people ask questions, you provide answers. When others make requests, you grant or reject their requests. When certain topics arise in conversation, you should weave your contributions to that topic and avoid tangents. Similarly, you should avoid dodging questions or abruptly changing topics because this is seen as uncooperative and, in some instances, may be seen as deceptive — especially if you change topics to avoid discussing something you want to keep hidden (McCornack, 2008).

Being Clear

Using clear language means presenting information in a straightforward way, rather than being obscure or ambiguous in your wording. For example, telling your mom that you like a recipe but that the food needs more salt makes a far clearer point than saying, "It's interesting." However, this does not mean we thoughtlessly dump offensive or hurtful information on others. Competent interpersonal communicators always consider others' feelings when designing their messages. When information is important and relevant to disclose, choose your words carefully to be both respectful *and* clear, so that others won't misconstrue your intended meaning.

Now that we have discussed the four characteristics of cooperative language, let's examine the second dimension of competent verbal communication: using "I" and "we" language.

"I" AND "WE" LANGUAGE

Competent verbal communicators take ownership of the things they say to others, especially when they must express negative feelings or criticism. One way to do this is by avoiding **"you" language**, or focusing attention and blame on other people, such as "*You* let us down." Instead, use **"I" language**: phrases that emphasize ownership of your feelings, opinions, and beliefs. For example, instead of saying "You hurt me," say "I'm feeling hurt." This difference may strike you as minor, but it has powerful effects: "I" language is less likely to trigger defensiveness in listeners compared to "you" language (Kubany, Richard, Bauer, & Muraoka, 1992). "I" language also creates a clearer impression that you're responsible for what you're saying and expressing your own perceptions rather than stating unquestionable truths.

Test This One Yourself

The next time you are in a challenging communication encounter in which you need to convey criticism or negative information, choose "I" rather than "you" language. Think of different ways you can use "I" language and explore how simple word choices can completely alter an interaction.

Using "we" language expresses your connection to others. In a sense, "we" language is the inverse of "I" language. "We" language helps bolster feelings of connection, collaboration, and similarity with other people. For example, when we teach together, we often use "we" language in talking with our class to build unity, such as "Next, *we* will consider the importance of nonverbal communication." As another example, go back and reread the preceding paragraphs of this chapter. You'll see that we use "we" language frequently, so that you—the readers—feel more connected to us—the authors!

NONVERBAL COMMUNICATION

Nonverbal communication is the intentional or unintentional transmission of meaning through an individual's *nonspoken* physical and behavioral cues (Patterson, 1995). Sometimes we do things like yawn, sigh, or grimace and mean nothing by them. But others may interpret them as acts of communication, and their perceptions lead them to respond in ways that affect us, our interpersonal communication, and our relationships. A boss who catches you yawning may express concern that you're "not paying attention," even though you're closely attending to your work. At other times, we intentionally craft nonverbal behaviors to communicate information to others. We add frowning bitmojis and emoticons ☹ to texts and e-mails to show family members we're sad, or smile as a form of greeting. We use touch to signal sympathy or affection, and move closer or farther away from others to indicate intimacy or emotional distance.

You can greatly strengthen your nonverbal communication skills—and your interpersonal communication competence—by better understanding four specific types of **nonverbal communication**.

COMMUNICATING THROUGH BODY MOVEMENTS

The first type of nonverbal communication is physical movement of the body, specifically facial expressions, eye contact, gestures, and body postures.

Facial Expressions
The face plays a pivotal role in shaping our perception of others. Think how much is communicated by a smile versus a frown. In fact, some scholars argue that facial expressions rank first among all forms of communication in their influence on our interpersonal impressions (Knapp & Hall, 2002). Our facial expressions communicate an endless stream of emotions, and we discern what others are feeling by assessing their expressions.

Eye Contact

Eye contact accomplishes many functions during interpersonal communication. We use our eyes to emote, signal turns at talk, and demonstrate that we're listening to others. When we share eye contact with another, we convey our interest in conversation or relationship intimacy, such as by locking eyes with a romantic partner.

Gestures

Gestures are hand and arm motions used to communicate messages (Streek, 1993). We commonly use four types of gestures. With *emblems*, the gesture and its verbal meaning are interchangeable. We can say "up" or point up and send the same message. Unlike emblems, *illustrators* accent or mime verbal messages. As you describe a rough road you recently biked, you bounce your hand up and down to illustrate the ride. *Regulators* control the exchange of conversational turns during interpersonal encounters, such as when you point a finger while trying to interrupt or hold your palm straight up to keep a person from interrupting (Rosenfeld, 1987). Finally, *adaptors* are touching gestures that serve a psychological or physical purpose (Ekman & Friesen, 1969). For example, you smooth your hair to make a better impression while meeting a potential new romantic partner.

Posture

Bodily posture includes straightness of back (erect or slouched), body lean (forward, backward, or vertical), straightness of shoulders (firm and broad or slumped), and head position (tilted or straight up). Your posture communicates many messages to others. For example, you can convey confidence simply by straightening your spine, bringing your head up, and pulling your shoulders back. Similarly, you can convey weakness and vulnerability by doing the opposite: curving your spine forward, bringing chin toward your chest, and letting your shoulders slump toward each other.

One of the most powerful messages posture conveys is **immediacy**: the degree to which you find someone interesting and attractive (Mehrabian, 1972). Want to nonverbally communicate that you like someone? Lean forward, keep your back straight, your arms open, and position your head up and facing toward the person when talking. Want to convey dislike? Lean back, close your arms, and look away.

COMMUNICATING THROUGH VOICE

The second type of nonverbal communication is voice. In her portrayal of a demanding boss in the movie *The Devil Wears Prada*, actress Meryl Streep adopted a voice that conveyed power, contempt, and a withering lack of warmth. Such examples illustrate the multifunctional nature of voice and that people's voices are intricate combinations of four characteristics: *tone, pitch, loudness,* and *speech rate.* Each of these can be used to communicate messages.

Tone

Tone is the most complex of human vocal characteristics, combining both richness and breathiness. For example, in a formal presentation, you can convey authority, controlling your vocal tone by allowing your voice to resonate deep in your chest and throat to achieve a full, rich tone. In contrast, letting your voice resonate through your sinus cavity creates a more nasal and whiny tone—often unpleasant to hear. Use of breath also affects tone. If you expel a great deal of air when speaking, you convey sexiness. If you constrict the airflow when speaking, you create a "thin" and "hard" tone that may communicate nervousness or anxiety.

Pitch

Pitch is the frequency of a speaker's voice: high, medium, or low. People tend to associate lower pitch—such as Darth Vader's voice—with strength, and higher pitch—such as the voice of SpongeBob SquarePants—with weakness. Not coincidentally, given negative gender stereotypes about "men being strong" and "women being weak," people believe that women have higher-pitched voices than men and that women's voices are more "shrill" and "whining" (Spender, 1990). Although women across cultures do use higher pitch than men, most men are capable of using a higher pitch than they normally do but *choose* to intentionally limit their range to lower pitch levels to convey strength (Brend, 1975).

Loudness

Loudness is the volume of your voice, and this too impacts impressions. You can use a louder volume on certain words to emphasize them, or drop your volume altogether to make the conversation seem more intimate. Volume plays such an important role in conveying meanings that people mimic it online by USING CAPITAL LETTERS TO EMPHASIZE CERTAIN POINTS. Indeed, people who communicate this way online sometimes are scolded for "shouting" or being "too loud."

Speech Rate

The final vocal characteristic is the speed at which you speak. Talking at a moderate and steady rate is often considered a critical technique for effective speaking. Public-speaking educators urge students to "slow down," and people in conversations often reduce their speech rate if they believe that their listeners don't understand them. But MIT computer science researcher Jean Krause found that speech rate is not the primary determinant of intelligibility (Krause, 2001). Instead, it's pronunciation and articulation of words. People who speak quickly but enunciate clearly are perceived just as competent as those who speak moderately or slowly.

COMMUNICATING THROUGH TOUCH

The third type of nonverbal communication, touch, is likely the first sense we develop in the womb, and receiving touch is a critical part of infant development (Knapp & Hall, 2002). Infants deprived of affectionate touch walk and talk later than others and suffer impaired emotional development in adulthood (Montagu, 1971).

Cultural upbringing has a strong impact on how people use and perceive touching. For example, many Hispanics more frequently use touch to convey friendship and warmth of feelings than do Europeans and Euro-Americans. Researchers in one study monitored casual conversations occurring in outdoor cafés in two different locales: San Juan, Puerto Rico, and London, England. They then averaged the number of touches between conversational partners (Environmental Protection Agency, 2002). The Puerto Ricans touched each other an average of 180 times per hour. The British average? Zero.

PUT IT TOGETHER

Consider how your feelings and emotions influence each of the four characteristics of how you communicate with your voice. For example, how does anxiety influence your speech rate? How does fear affect your volume? What can you do to help modulate your voice when you are experiencing feelings or emotions?

Because people differ in their comfort both giving and receiving touch, consider adapting your use of touch to others' preferences, letting the other person be your guide. If you are talking with a person who repeatedly touches your arm gently while talking, you can probably presume that such a mild form of touch would be acceptable to reciprocate. However, if a person offers you no touch at all, not even a greeting handshake, you would be wise to inhibit your touching.

COMMUNICATING THROUGH PERSONAL SPACE

The final type of nonverbal communication we discuss in this book is how we physically distance ourselves from each other. Scholars distinguish four communication distances: intimate, personal, social, and public. Each distance conveys something different regarding relationships (Hall, 1966). **Intimate space** ranges from 0 to 18 inches. Sharing intimate space with someone is a defining nonverbal feature of close relationships. **Personal space** ranges between 18 inches and 4 feet and is the distance we occupy during encounters with friends. For most Americans and Canadians, personal space is about your "wingspan" — that is, the distance from fingertip to fingertip when you extend your arms. **Social space** ranges from about 4 to 12 feet. Many people use it when communicating in the workplace or with acquaintances and strangers. In **public space**, the distance between persons ranges upward from 12 feet, including great distances; this span occurs most often during formal occasions such as public speeches or college lectures.

How can we use personal space more competently? Keep in mind that North Americans' notions of personal space tend to be larger than those in most other cultures, especially people from Latin America or the Middle East. When interacting with people from other cultures, adjust your use of space in accordance with your conversational partner's preferences. Realize, also, that if you're from a culture that values large personal space, others will feel most comfortable interacting at a closer distance than you're used to. If you insist on maintaining a large personal space bubble around yourself when interacting with people from other cultures, they may think you're aloof, you're distant, or you don't want to talk with them.

Now that we have explored dimensions of both verbal and nonverbal communication, let's turn our focus to examine another aspect of competent interpersonal communication: the critical process of listening.

LISTENING

We often take listening for granted. Compared with the knowledge, motivation, and skill that competent speaking requires, listening seems to just happen. But viewing listening as secondary to speaking misses two truths. First, listening is our most primal and primary communication skill. As children, we develop the ability to listen long before we learn how to speak, read, or write. As adults, we spend more time listening than in any other type of communication activity (Wolvin & Coakley, 1996). Second, we each have the potential to develop our listening into something far more profound than passive action. When we practice *active listening*, we transcend our own thoughts, ideas, and beliefs, and begin to directly experience the words and worlds of others (McNaughton, Hamlin, McCarthy, Head-Reeves, & Schreiner, 2007). By focusing our attention, tailoring our listening to the situation, and letting others know we understand them, we move beyond the personal and create the *interpersonal*. The result is improved relationships (Bunkers, 2010).

The process of listening unfolds over time, rather than instantaneously, through five steps: receiving, attending, understanding, responding, and recalling.

SELF-QUIZ

Assessing Your Listening Abilities

Read each statement. Place a check mark next to those you agree with.

Considering how I interact with others in my daily life, I:

Receiving

_____ am aware of external noise and how it impacts an encounter

_____ use both my eyes and ears to help me listen

_____ use ear plugs to protect my hearing in noisy settings

Attending

_____ put away my cell phone when I am speaking to someone face-to-face

_____ focus my attention on the single task of listening to the other person

_____ concentrate on the words that are spoken by the other person

_____ notice the nonverbal cues the other person is using

Understanding

_____ attempt to understand information by linking it to a variety of concepts I already know

_____ try to resist making the fundamental attribution error

_____ refrain from forming snap judgments

_____ try to see the situation from the other person's perspective

Responding

_____ look directly at the other person who is speaking

_____ provide the other person with cues to indicate my interest, such as nodding my head or saying "yes"

_____ let the other person know when I do not understand what was communicated

_____ know when I need to paraphrase to indicate my understanding to another person

Recalling

_____ take notes when necessary to help my memory

_____ try to listen with all my senses

_____ use methods to help me remember a person, such as linking their name to where we first met

Scoring: Count the number of check marks you made. Totals of 0–6 = low LA; 7–12 = moderate LA; 13 and above = high LA.

RECEIVING

While walking to class, you unexpectedly run into a good friend and stop to chat. As she talks, you listen to her words as well as observe her behavior. But how does this process happen? As you observe your friend, light reflects off her skin, clothes, and hair and travels through the lens of your eye to your retina, which contains optic nerves. These nerves become stimulated, sending information to your brain, which translates the information into visual images, such as your friend smiling or shaking her head, an effect called **seeing**. At the same time, sound waves generated by her voice enter your inner ear, causing your eardrum to vibrate. These vibrations travel along acoustic nerves to your brain, which interprets them as your friend's words and voice tone, an effect known as **hearing**.

Together, seeing and hearing constitute **receiving**, the first step in the listening process. Receiving is critical to listening — we can't listen if we don't "see" or hear the other person. Unfortunately, our abilities to receive often are hampered by *noise pollution*, sound in the surrounding environment that obscures or distracts our attention from auditory input. Sources of noise pollution include crowds, road and air traffic, construction equipment, and music.

You can enhance your ability to receive — and improve your listening — by becoming aware of noise pollution and adjusting your interactions accordingly. Practice monitoring the noise level in your environment during your interpersonal encounters and notice how it impedes your listening. When possible, avoid interactions in loud and noisy environments, or move to quieter locations for important conversations. And if you enjoy loud music or live concerts, always use ear protection to ensure your auditory safety.

ATTENDING

Attending, the second step in the listening process, involves devoting attention to the information you've received. Without first attending to information, we can't interpret, understand, or respond to it (Kahneman, 1973).

To improve attention, try limiting your **multitasking**: using multiple forms of technology at once, each feeding an unrelated information stream (Ophir, Nass, & Wagner, 2012). An example of multitasking is writing a class paper on your computer while also listening to music and using social media. Stanford psychologist Clifford Nass has found that habitual multitaskers are extremely confident in their abilities to perform at peak levels on the tasks they simultaneously juggle (Glenn, 2010). But their confidence is misplaced. Multitaskers perform substantially *worse* on tasks, compared with individuals who focus their attention on a single task only (Ophir, Nass, & Wagner, 2012). Not surprisingly, habitual multitaskers have grave difficulty listening, as listening requires extended attention (Carr, 2010). We can train our brains to sustain attention by limiting multitasking and spending some time each day focused on one task (such as reading, listening to music, or engaging in prayer or meditation).

UNDERSTANDING

Understanding involves interpreting the meaning of another's communication by comparing newly received information against our past knowledge (Macrae & Bodenhausen, 2001). When we receive and attend to new information, we place it in **short-term memory** to temporarily house it as we make sense of its meaning. While the new information sits in short-term memory, we call up relevant knowledge from **long-term memory**, the permanent information storage areas of our minds. We then create understanding by comparing relevant prior knowledge from long-term memory to this new information in short-term memory.

RESPONDING

Listening requires more than simply receiving, attending, and understanding. We also convey these actions to the person who is speaking *while* he or she is speaking. How? By doing things like nodding our head, smiling, and saying "Uh-huh" and "Yeah."

Although most listeners respond in these ways, **active listeners** set themselves apart from those who merely "listen" by doing three things when they respond: *providing positive feedback*, *paraphrasing*, and *clarifying* (McNaughton et al., 2007).

Positive Feedback
We provide feedback when we use verbal and nonverbal behaviors to communicate attention and understanding *while* others are talking. Scholars distinguish between two kinds of feedback: positive and negative (Wolvin & Coakley, 1996). **Positive feedback** includes looking directly at the person speaking, smiling, positioning your body to face the speaker, and leaning forward. The combination of these behaviors indicates to speakers that you're actively listening. In contrast, people who use negative feedback send a very different message to speakers: "I'm not interested in paying attention to you or understanding what you're saying." Behaviors that convey negative feedback include avoiding eye contact, turning your body away, and looking bored or distracted.

To effectively display positive feedback during interpersonal encounters, try four simple suggestions (Barker, 1971; Daly, 1975). First, *make your feedback obvious*. As communication scholar John Daly notes, no matter how actively you listen, unless others perceive your feedback, they won't view you as actively listening. Second, *make your feedback appropriate*. Different situations, speakers, and messages require more or less intensity of positive feedback. Third, *make your feedback clear* by avoiding behaviors that might be mistaken as negative feedback. For example, something as simple as innocently stealing a glance at your phone to check the time might unintentionally suggest that you're bored or wish the person would stop speaking. Finally, always *provide feedback quickly* in response to what the speaker has just said.

Paraphrasing and Clarifying

Active listeners also communicate attention and understanding by saying things *after* their conversational partners have finished their turns—making it clear that they were listening. One way to do this is by **paraphrasing**, summarizing others' comments after they have finished ("My read on your message is that . . . " or "You seem to be saying that . . ."). This practice allows you to verify the accuracy of your understanding during both face-to-face and online encounters. Use paraphrasing judiciously, however, as some conversational partners may find frequent paraphrasing annoying.

Of course, on some occasions, we simply don't understand what others have said. In such instances, it's perfectly appropriate to engage in **clarifying**, asking for additional explanation regarding the person's intended meaning. Try saying, "I'm sorry, but I'm not sure I understood you. Could you please explain that again?" This technique not only helps you clarify the meaning of what you're hearing, it also enables you to communicate your desire to understand the other person.

RECALLING

The final stage of listening is **recalling**, remembering information after you've received, attended to, understood, and responded to it. Recalling is a crucial part of the listening process because the effectiveness of our listening is determined by our abilities to accurately recall information after we've heard it. Think about it: when a romantic partner asks, "Were you listening to me?," we typically provide evidence of our active listening by reciting a list of everything that the partner said.

How can you boost your recall ability? Because listening is rooted in both visual and auditory information and memory is enhanced by using all five senses, we can bolster our memories by creating sensory "tabs" to help us access the information. For example, we can link information to pleasant or even silly visuals, scents, or sounds. Try journaling visual images of an interpersonal encounter by writing detailed notes, doodles, or diagrams to document the contents of a conversation. You also could link a new acquaintance's name with a unique physical feature to help visualize the person. Finally, when you develop notes or write in a journal, review your writings repeatedly, including reciting them out loud, because auditory repetition aids memory.

 GAUGE YOUR KNOWLEDGE

Before proceeding to the next chapter, refer back to the chapter-opening checklist to assess your understanding of the chapter concepts.

Interpersonal Relationships   *4*

Now that we have laid the foundation for you to enhance your interpersonal communication and listening skills, we consider the types of relationships to which you may apply these skills. In this chapter, we delve into the distinguishing features of three different types of relationships and methods for maintaining them.

By the end of this chapter, you should be able to:

YOUR CHAPTER-OPENING CHECKLIST

- ✓ List two components determining interpersonal relational success.
- ✓ Distinguish liking from loving.
- ✓ Explain Social Exchange Theory.
- ✓ Differentiate equity from inequity.
- ✓ Describe three relationship types.
- ✓ Define romantic relationship.
- ✓ Explain the four elements of romantic relationships.
- ✓ Define commitment.
- ✓ Define family.
- ✓ Describe the six characteristics of family.
- ✓ Define friendship.
- ✓ Recognize the five characteristics of friendships.
- ✓ Define relational maintenance.
- ✓ Distinguish the four categories of relational maintenance.

RELATIONSHIP FOUNDATIONS

Interpersonal relationships are the emotional, mental, and physical involvements that we forge with others through our communication. Many factors determine whether interpersonal relationships form, thrive, and survive, including similarity, physical proximity, and physical attractiveness. But two of the biggest determinants of interpersonal relationship success are the degree to which liking and loving are present and the balance of rewards and costs exchanged between the relationship partners. Let's explore each of these components and how they impact relationship health and satisfaction.

LIKING AND LOVING

At the core of whether we create and continue interpersonal relationships are the positive feelings of connection we feel toward others. These feelings often manifest as *liking* and *loving*. Although many people think of liking and loving as interwoven — loving just being a more intense gradation of liking — most scholars agree that liking and loving are separate emotional states, with different causes and outcomes (Berscheid & Regan, 2005).

Specifically, **liking** is a feeling of affection and respect that we have for another person (Rubin, 1973). *Affection* is a sense of warmth and fondness toward that person, whereas *respect* is admiration for that person apart from how he or she treats and communicates with you. As we will discuss in more detail shortly, liking is central to friendships: our closest friends typically are people whose company we enjoy, and who we "look up to" in some regard — that is, they inspire us to be better people. But liking also is a cornerstone of successful romantic involvements and may distinguish between family members who you feel close to versus those you don't. For instance, how many of your relatives do you truly enjoy and admire, versus those who you merely tolerate (and perhaps quietly wonder, how could I possibly be related to this person?)?

Loving, in contrast, is a vastly deeper and more intense emotional commitment that consists of three components: intimacy, caring, and attachment (Rubin, 1973). *Intimacy* is a feeling of closeness and "union" between you and your partner (Mashek & Aron, 2004). *Caring* is the concern you have for your partner's welfare and the desire to keep your partner happy. *Attachment* is a longing to be in your partner's presence as much as possible. Loving is characteristic of romantic love: we feel bonded to our lovers; concerned about their happiness; and driven to be with them, emotionally and physically. But we also may "love" (in this definitional sense) family and friends as well — depending on how deeply we feel intimacy, caring, and attachment toward them. For instance, if you have a best friend to whom you feel deeply connected, or a sibling whom you miss whenever you're separated for a period of time, it's likely that you love these people. The inverse also is true: if you feel no strong desire to be with someone, aren't especially concerned about his or her wellbeing, and don't feel any strong emotional connection, it's likely that you don't love this person.

EXCHANGE OF RESOURCES

The second foundational component of interpersonal relationships is what partners give and receive from each other within the domain of their relationship. All relationships revolve around the resources that people exchange that compel them to initially form and subsequently stay or leave. **Social exchange theory** proposes that we forge and continue relationships with those we see as offering substantial rewards (resources we like and want) with few associated costs (things demanded of us in return). Two specific standards drive our relational evaluations: whether we perceive the partner as providing us with the rewards *we think we deserve* in this type of relationship (e.g., affection, emotional support, companionship, money, sex, etc.), and whether we perceive these rewards as *superior to those we could get elsewhere* (Kelley & Thibaut, 1978). In simple terms, you're driven to be with people who give you what you want and who provide better rewards than others.

But it's not simply whether someone offers you a good "cost–reward ratio" that determines relationship formation and stability. Your perception of **equity**, the balance of rewards and costs exchanged between you and the other person, also is important. People in close relationships have a strong sense of **proportional justice**: the balance between benefits gained from the relationship versus contributions made to the relationship (Hatfield, 1983). And people are happiest when this balance is approximately equal (Sprecher, 2001). **Inequity** occurs when the benefits or contributions provided by one person are greater than those provided by the other. People who get more rewards from their relationships for fewer costs than their partners are *overbenefited*; those who get fewer rewards from their relationships for more costs than their partners are *underbenefited*. Overbenefited individuals experience negative emotions, such as guilt, while underbenefited partners experience emotions, such as sadness and anger (Sprecher, 2001).

Equity and inequity strongly determine the short- and long-term success of both friendships and romantic relationships (Stafford, 2003). Friendships typically won't survive if the friends view the relationship as "unfair" in terms of what each is giving versus getting. The same holds true for romance: one study found that only 23 percent of equitable romances broke up during a several-month period, whereas 54 percent of inequitable romantic relationships broke up (Sprecher, 2001).

For family relationships, however, creating and sustaining equity often can be difficult. Many parents struggle to treat each child equally. However, the "balance sheet" between parents and children will *never* be equal: parents usually give more to children than they ever will get back in return, in terms of objective rewards.

Now that we have explored two components linked to interpersonal relational success, let's examine three different types of interpersonal relationships.

RELATIONSHIP TYPES

As many different types of interpersonal relationships exist as there are people to create them. At the forefront of our emotional lives, however, are three relationship types that tend to eclipse others in terms of their importance: romantic involvements, family relationships, and friendships.

ROMANTIC RELATIONSHIPS

We know that liking differs from loving, that people exchange resources in relationships, and that equitable exchange is important. But what exactly does it mean to have a *romantic* relationship? A **romantic relationship** is a chosen interpersonal involvement forged through communication in which the participants perceive the bond as romantic. *Four elements* of romantic relationships underlie this definition. First, a romantic relationship exists whenever the partners perceive that it does. As perceptions change, so too does the relationship. For example, a couple may consider their relationship "casual dating" but still define it as "romantic" (rather than friendly). Or, a long-term couple may feel more companionate than passionate but still consider themselves "in love." If two partners' perceptions of their relationship differ — for example, one person feels romantic and the other does not — they do not have a romantic relationship (Miller & Steinberg, 1975).

Second, romantic relationships exhibit remarkable diversity in the ages and genders of the partners as well as in their ethnic and religious backgrounds and sexual orientations. Despite this diversity, most relationships function in similar ways. Consider sexual orientation. Whether a romantic relationship is between lesbian, gay, or straight partners, the individuals involved place the same degree of importance on their relationship, devote similar amounts of time and energy to maintaining their bond, and demonstrate similar openness in their communication (Haas & Stafford, 2005). The exact same factors that determine marital success between men and women (such as honesty, loyalty, commitment, and dedication to maintenance) also predict stability and satisfaction within same-sex couples (Kurdek, 2005). As relationship scholar Sharon Brehm summarizes, gay and lesbian couples "fall in love in the same way, feel the same passions, experience the same doubts, and feel the same commitments as straights" (Brehm, Miller, Perlman, & Campbell, 2002, p. 27).

Third, we choose our romantic relationships, selecting not only with whom we initiate involvements but also whether and how we maintain these bonds. Thus, contrary to widespread belief, love doesn't "strike us out of the blue" or "sweep us away." Choice plays a role even in arranged marriages: the spouses' families and social networks select an appropriate partner, and in many cases the betrothed retain at least some control over whether the choice is acceptable (Hendrick & Hendrick, 1992).

Finally, romantic relationships often involve **commitment**: a strong psychological attachment to a partner and an intention to continue the relationship long into the future (Arriaga & Agnew, 2001). When you forge a commitment with a partner, positive outcomes often result. Commitment leads couples to work harder on maintaining their relationships, resulting in greater satisfaction (Rusbult, Arriaga, & Agnew, 2001). Commitment also reduces the likelihood that partners will cheat sexually when separated by geographic distance (Le, Korn, Crockett, & Loving, 2010). And although men are stereotyped in the media as "commitment-phobic," this is false. *Both* men and women view commitment as an important part of romantic relationships (Miller, Perlman, & Brehm, 2007).

FAMILY RELATIONSHIPS

Families have a primacy that no other relationships rival. Family members are the first people we see, hear, touch, and interact with. As we grow from infancy to childhood, we learn from family the most basic of skills: how to walk, talk, feed, and clothe ourselves. As we develop further, our families teach us deeper lessons about life: the importance of support, honesty, sacrifice, and love. And as our relationships broaden to include friendships and romances, we still use kinship as a metaphor to describe closeness: "How close are we? We're like *family!*" (Rubin, 1996). But with family comes obligations. We don't *choose* our families — we are brought into them by birth, adopted into them by law, or integrated into them by remarriage. And when problems arise in our families, the stress also is unrivalled. A survey of adults asking them the greatest source of emotional strain in the preceding day found the most frequent answer was "family" (Warr & Payne, 1982). When the same sample was asked the greatest source of pleasure from the previous day, the answer was identical: "family." Day in and day out, family relationships provide us with our greatest joys and most bitter heartaches (Myers, 2002).

Family is a network of people who share their lives over long periods of time and are bound by marriage, blood, or commitment; who consider themselves as family; and who share a significant history and anticipated future of functioning in a family relationship (Galvin, Brommel, & Bylund, 2004). This definition highlights *six characteristics* that distinguish families from other social groups.

First, families possess a strong sense of family identity, created by how they communicate (Braithwaite et al., 2010). The way you talk with family members, the stories you exchange, and even the manner in which members of your family handle conflict all contribute to a shared sense of what your family is like (Tovares, 2010).

Second, families use communication to define boundaries, both inside the family and to distinguish family members from outsiders (Afifi, 2003; Koerner & Fitzpatrick, 2006). Some families constrict information that flows out ("Don't talk about our family problems with anyone else"). Some also restrict physical access to the family — for example, by dictating with whom family members can become romantically involved ("No son of mine is going to marry a Protestant!"). Others set few such boundaries. For instance, a family may welcome friends and neighbors as unofficial members, such as an "uncle" or "aunt" who isn't really related to your parents (Braithwaite et al., 2010). A family may even welcome others' children, such as the friendly neighbors across the street whom you think of as your "family away from home." And if remarriage occurs and stepfamilies form, these boundaries are renegotiated (Golish, 2003).

Third, the emotional bonds underlying family relationships are intense and complex. Family members typically hold both warm *and* antagonistic feelings toward one another (Silverstein & Giarrusso, 2010). As author Lillian Rubin (1996) notes, family relationships have "an elemental quality that touches the deepest layers of our inner life and stirs our most primitive emotional responses" (p. 256). Consider the strength of feeling that arises in you when you get into an argument with a parent or sibling, or when you celebrate an important milestone (a graduation, a wedding, a new job).

Fourth, families share a history (Galvin et al., 2004). Such histories can stretch back for generations and feature family members from an array of cultures. These histories often set expectations regarding how family members should behave. For example, when Steve was growing up, a routine parental message regarding behavior was "McCornacks don't *do* that!" Families also share a common future: they expect to maintain their bonds indefinitely. For better or worse, everything you say and do becomes a part of your family history, shaping future interactions and determining whether your family relationships are healthy or destructive.

Fifth, family members may share genetic material (Crosnoe & Cavanagh, 2010). This can lead to shared physical characteristics as well as similar personalities, outlooks on life, mental abilities, and ways of relating to others. For example, some studies suggest that interpersonal inclinations such as shyness and aggressiveness are influenced by genes (Carducci & Zimbardo, 1995).

Finally, family members constantly juggle multiple and sometimes competing roles (Silverstein & Giarrusso, 2010). Within your family, you're not just a daughter or son, but perhaps a sibling, a spouse, or an aunt or uncle as well. By the time you reach middle age, you simultaneously may be a parent, spouse, grandparent, daughter or son, *and* sibling—and each of these roles carries with it varying expectations and demands. This makes communicating competently within families challenging.

FRIENDSHIPS

Friendships are an important source of emotional security and self-esteem (Rawlins, 1992) and play a crucial role in our lives. Friendships facilitate a sense of belonging when we're young, help solidify our identity during adolescence, and provide satisfaction and social support as we age (Miller, Hefner, & Scott, 2007). But what exactly *is* friendship? **Friendship** is a voluntary interpersonal relationship characterized by intimacy and liking (McEwan, Babin Gallagher, & Farinelli, 2008). Whether it's casual or close, short or long term, friendships have several distinguishing characteristics.

First, compared to other types of relationships, we have greater liberty in choosing our friends (Sias et al., 2008). Whether a friendship forms is largely determined by the people involved and is based on their mutual desire to create such a relationship. This sharply differs from our romantic and family involvements. For example, you may face substantial familial or cultural constraints in your choice of romantic partners, limited by their age, gender, ethnicity, religion, or income level. You may even have a spouse chosen *for* you in an arranged marriage. Similarly, you are bound to your family through no choice of your own, but rather by the involuntary ties of birth, adoption, or the creation of a stepfamily. As French poet Jacques Delille (1738–1813) stated, "Fate chooses your relations, you choose your friends."

Second, the primary force that draws us to our friends is similarity (Parks & Floyd, 1996). This is true across ages, genders, sexual orientations, and ethnicities. One outcome of this is that as our interests and activities change, so will our friendships. If your political or religious beliefs shift, or an injury prevents you from playing a beloved sport, friendships related to those things also may change. Some will endure—shifting their focus to new points of commonality—but others will fade away. One of the most common reasons for ending friendships is because interests and beliefs that once were shared now have changed (Miller, Hefner, & Scott, 2007).

Third, friendships are defined through disclosure. Both men and women report that being able to freely and deeply disclose is *the* defining feature of friendship (Parks & Floyd, 1996). Self-disclosure between friends means sharing private thoughts and feelings and believing that "we can tell each other anything." The relationship between friendship and self-disclosure is reciprocal, as well. The more you consider someone a friend, the more you will disclose; the more you disclose, the more you will consider that person a friend (Shelton, Trail, West, & Bergsieker, 2010).

Fourth, as noted earlier in this chapter, friendships are rooted in *liking* (Rubin, 1973). Because friendships are rooted in liking—rather than love—we're not as emotionally attached to our friends as we are to other intimates, and we're not as emotionally demanding of them. Correspondingly, we're expected to be more loyal to and more willing to help romantic partners and family members compared to friends (Davis & Todd, 1985).

Finally, friendships are less stable, more likely to change, and easier to break off than family or romantic relationships (Johnson, Wittenberg, Villagran, Mazur, & Villagran, 2003). Why is this? Consider the differences in depth of commitment. We're bonded to friends by choice, rooted in shared interests. But we're bonded to families by social and legal commitment and to lovers by deep emotional and sexual attachment. These loyalties mean we may choose or forgo professional opportunities to preserve romances or stay close to family. But most of us will choose to pursue our careers over staying geographically close to friends (Patterson, 2007).

Now that we have examined three types of interpersonal relationships, let's investigate methods for maintaining our relationships.

PUT IT TOGETHER

Choose one of your friendships. Using the standards of social exchange theory, evaluate it in terms of what you think you deserve, what you think you could get in a different friendship, and equity.

RELATIONSHIP MAINTENANCE

Many people believe that if relationships are "meant to be," then happiness will just happen. They disregard the idea that we must invest effort into every relationship if we want it to continue. A basic rule of relationships is that maintenance is necessary to keep them from deteriorating (Stafford, 2003). Relationships, in this sense, resemble other long-term investments, such as cars, bodies, or houses; without routine maintenance, they *will* fall apart. **Relational maintenance** refers to using communication and supportive behaviors to sustain a desired relationship status and level of satisfaction (Stafford, Dainton, & Haas, 2000). Communication scholar Laura Stafford observed four methods that people in happy relationships routinely use to maintain their relationships, regardless of their ethnicity, sexual orientation, or type of relationship (romance, family, or friendship): positivity, assurances, disclosure, and sharing tasks (Stafford, 2010).

SELF-QUIZ

How Do You Approach Relational Maintenance?

Read each statement. Place a check mark next to those you agree with.

Considering how I approach my relationship, I:

Positivity

_____ surprise the other person with small gifts

_____ compliment the other person

_____ do favors to help out the other person when I can

_____ try to communicate in an optimistic and positive way

Assurances

_____ directly tell the other person how important he or she is to me

_____ prioritize my relationship over other obligations on my time

_____ directly tell the other person how much I value our relationship

_____ talk with the other person about our future together

Self-Disclosure

_____ attempt to cultivate a respectful relationship

_____ reveal my worries to the other person

_____ openly share my feelings and emotions with the other person

_____ encourage the other person to share his or her thoughts with me

Shared Tasks

_____ strive to do tasks before I am asked to do them

_____ do my fair share of the work in a relationship

_____ help out with errands

_____ ask the other person what I can do to help

Scoring: The category with the most check marks indicates how you primarily approach relational maintenance. If you score equally high on two or more different approaches, you use more than one approach.

POSITIVITY

Positivity includes communicating in a cheerful, sunny, and optimistic fashion; doing unsolicited favors; and giving unexpected gifts. People in close family and friendship relationships, and gay, lesbian, and straight romances, cite positivity as *the* most important maintenance tactic for ensuring happiness (Dainton & Stafford, 1993; Haas & Stafford, 2005; Stafford, 2010).

We cultivate positivity by attempting to create enjoyable and upbeat interactions, bolstering others with compliments or gifts, and by being considerate and thoughtful of others. Examples include texting a family member a "have a wonderful day" message, treating a friend to a surprise lunch out, or sending flowers for no reason at all to a lover. We undercut positivity when we fixate upon and complain about problems without offering solutions; whine, pout, and sulk when we don't get our way; or belittle favors and gifts from a partner.

ASSURANCES

We all like to feel wanted, needed, and loved. So it's no surprise that a key maintenance tactic in boosting relationship satisfaction is **assurances**: messages that emphasize how much a partner means to you, emphasize how important the relationship is, and ensure a secure future together. We can express assurances directly or indirectly. Direct examples include saying, "I love you" to a lover, "I want us to ALWAYS be best friends!" to a friend, or "I'm SO glad that you're my sister!" to a sibling. Indirect examples emphasize the value you place on your time together, such as texting "I can't wait to see you again," or "I'm really looking forward to being home and hanging with y'all over spring break" (Rabby, 1997). We undercut assurances by flirting with others in front of a lover, telling a friend how much you like your *other* friends, or telling a family member that you wish you were part of a different family.

SELF-DISCLOSURE

A third maintenance strategy is creating a climate of security and trust within your family, friendship, or romantic relationship, so that each person feels like he or she can engage in **self-disclosure** (see definition in Chapter 2). To foster self-disclosure, we must behave in ways that are predictable, trustworthy, and ethical so that we feel comfortable disclosing fears and feelings without repercussion. Consistently behaving this way over time fosters mutual respect and the perception that self-disclosure will be welcomed. Examples of self-disclosure include revealing your fears and vulnerabilities to your partner, sharing your feelings and emotions with your family, encouraging your friend to disclose his or her thoughts and feelings, and offering empathy in return. In contrast, we undercut self-disclosure when we disparage another's perspective, refuse to share important information with your partner, or betray a friend by divulging confidential information about him or her with others.

SHARING TASKS

The final form of maintenance is the least glamorous—but also the most frequently practiced. All relationships have practical tasks that must be done—whether it's bills to be paid, children to be taken care of, or assistance in times of need or emergency (such as a ride to work when a car breaks down). **Sharing tasks** is taking mutual responsibility for practical demands that arise in our lives and negotiating an equitable division of labor. Although this may sound like something that only serious, cohabiting, or married couples face, sharing tasks is relevant for *all* relationship types and includes responsibilities like providing transportation to work or campus, running errands, and making reservations for dinner. We share tasks when we pitch in equally on everyday responsibilities, ask our families how we can help out, and make an effort to handle tasks before being asked to do them by another. We undercut task sharing by strategically avoiding our share of the work, neglecting to inquire how we can help others, or expecting our partners to run errands and do things for us.

Test This One Yourself

Surprise a roommate or family member by cleaning up. Then see how they react. What type of emotional and relational outcomes occurred?

 GAUGE YOUR KNOWLEDGE

Before proceeding to the next chapter, refer back to the chapter-opening checklist to assess your understanding of the chapter concepts.

Interpersonal Challenges   **5**

Three of the most significant interpersonal communication challenges we face in our lives are addressing the inevitable tensions that arise in close relationships, successfully managing conflicts that surface, and skillfully offering empathy and support to others in their times of need. Now that we have established an understanding of the factors influencing your communication in different types of interpersonal relationships, we can apply your knowledge to these communication challenges. We begin by considering relationship tensions.

By the end of this chapter, you should be able to:

YOUR CHAPTER-OPENING CHECKLIST

✓ Define relational dialectics.

✓ Describe three common dialectic forms.

✓ Define conflict.

✓ Explain four characteristics of conflict.

✓ Describe kitchen-sinking.

✓ Distinguish between five conflict approaches.

✓ List two risks of avoidance.

✓ Explain two factors influencing accommodation.

✓ State two risks of competition.

✓ Describe four suggestions to facilitate collaboration.

✓ Define empathy.

✓ Define supportive communication.

✓ Distinguish competent from incompetent support.

✓ Recognize seven suggestions for improving supportive communication.

MANAGING RELATIONSHIP TENSIONS

One outcome of creating close interpersonal relationships is managing their dynamics. Regardless of the type of relationship, we often experience diverging impulses or competing tensions between ourselves and our feelings toward others. This is known as **relational dialectics** (Baxter, 1990). Relational dialectics take three common forms.

PUT IT TOGETHER

Choose one of the relational maintenance categories from our last chapter. Consider ways in which it could be used, and what you could say or do, to address the different relational effect.

OPENNESS VERSUS PROTECTION

The first is *openness versus protection*, or the contrasting desires to self-disclose information versus maintain privacy. For example, as romantic relationships become more intimate, we naturally exchange more personal information with our partners. In fact, many people see self-disclosure as the primary conduit to create closeness. Most of us enjoy the feeling of unity, connection, and mutual insight created through such sharing. While we want to be open with our partners, we also may feel the need to keep certain aspects of our selves — such as our *most* private thoughts and feelings — protected. Too much openness provokes an uncomfortable sense that we've lost our privacy and must share *everything* with our partners. This dialectic is especially pronounced between parents and teenagers, because it is during this time period in a child's development when friends begin replacing family as the primary providers of social support (Golish, 2000). For example, when each of our three sons was in elementary school, they were quite open about sharing their thoughts, feelings, and daily lives with us. Upon entering adolescence, however, they gradually began to pull back from self-disclosure, increasingly protecting their thoughts and feelings, to the point where we began to approach them like "oysters" — carefully prodding and gently prying loose their "pearls" of self-disclosure.

NOVELTY VERSUS PREDICTABILITY

The second dialectic occurs when our need for excitement and change pushes against our need for stability — known as *novelty versus predictability*. We all enjoy the security that accompanies knowing how our relationship partners will behave, how we'll behave, and how our relationships likely will unfold. But boredom commonly parallels predictability, especially within romantic relationships. The "passion" experienced in early romance is because our new partners have the ability to excite and surprise us in novel, interesting, and pleasing ways — keeping us a bit uncertain, but in a good way. However, as our knowledge and certainty about our partners increase over time, the novelty and excitement of the relationship diminish, and things may become increasingly monotonous. Reconciling the desire for predictability with the need for novelty is one of the most profound emotional challenges facing partners in romantic relationships. To help manage this challenge, try to learn and do new things so that you continue to grow as a person and evolve as a couple.

AUTONOMY VERSUS CONNECTION

The final dialectic is *autonomy versus connection* — or our competing desires to maintain our individual independence versus function as part of a pair or unit. We elect to form close relationships largely out of a desire to bond with other human beings. Yet if we come to feel so connected to others that our individual identity disappears, we may choose to pull back, rediscover, and reassert some of our autonomy. The autonomy–connection dialectic is especially pronounced within families. Even though you may feel intensely connected to your family, you probably also struggle to create your own separate identity. This may be true especially for younger siblings, who might mistakenly be called the name of their older siblings by their teachers, or for mothers, who may be addressed as someone's "mom" rather than by their first names. While we are comforted in knowing that we are connected to others, we also may resent the connections that seem to stifle our unique sense of "self."

How can we negotiate autonomy versus connection in our families? One way is to challenge yourself to take on some of the tasks that your family has fulfilled, learning to rely more on yourself or the assistance of people outside your family. Too much dependence on family — especially for tasks you could accomplish on your own — can erode your self-reliance, self-confidence, and independence (Strauss, 2006). Second, appraise your social networks (including your family) and assess the degree to which family members constitute the closest people in your life. If you have few or even no close ties with anyone outside of your family, you may feel less autonomous because of your dependence on your family. Likewise, lack of ties to your family can create a profound sense of independence but paltry emotional bonds with them.

Now that we have explored common dialectics in close relationships, let's consider how we can use our communication skills to manage conflict in these relationships.

HANDLING CONFLICT

The second challenge we face within close relationships is conflict. Although we may conceive of conflict as something "bad" or "wrong," conflict actually is a normal aspect of *all* relationships (Canary, 2003). Interacting with other people (and their unique goals, preferences, personalities, and opinions) means regularly having your wants and needs run up against theirs, triggering disputes (Malis & Roloff, 2006). On average, people report *seven* conflicts a week, mostly among relatives, friends, and lovers with whom they've argued before (Benoit &

Benoit, 1990). Thus, the challenge we face is not how to avoid conflict, or live a conflict-free life, but instead how to constructively manage the conflicts that inevitably *will* arise.

WHAT IS CONFLICT?

Take a minute and recall your most recent conflict. What was the topic? Almost any issue can spark conflict, including money, time, sex, religion, politics, love, or chores. And almost anyone can create conflict: family, friends, lovers, coworkers, teammates, casual acquaintances, or complete strangers. Despite these variations, all conflicts share similar attributes. **Conflict** is a process that occurs when people perceive they have incompatible goals or that someone is interfering in their ability to achieve their objectives (Wilmot & Hocker, 2010). Four features characterize most conflicts: they begin with perception, they involve clashes in goals or behaviors, they unfold over time as a process, and they are dynamic.

First, conflict begins with perception. As we know from Chapter 2, people often succumb to the fundamental attribution error, making internal rather than external judgments about people's behaviors. Given this tendency, it is not surprising that our perceptions regarding conflict may be skewed as well. Thus, a first step in handling conflict more effectively is to pause to consider the accuracy of your perceptions.

Second, conflict involves clashes in goals or behaviors (Zacchilli, Hendrick, & Hendrick, 2009). We can relate this back to the first feature, and say that people *perceive* incompatible goals or actions (Roloff & Soule, 2002). Some conflicts revolve around incompatible goals, ranging from everyday leisure disputes ("I want to go dancing!" vs. "I want to stay in and watch a movie!"), to serious personal values quarrels ("I want our children to be raised Jewish!" vs. "I want them to be raised Catholic!"). Other disputes develop when actions collide, such as a friend interrupting your studying with her repeated texts (which you ignore), or a manager demanding that you work late to cover for an employee who called in sick (which you refuse to do because you have concert tickets that night).

Third, although people often describe conflict as a series of unrelated events ("I sent her this carefully worded text, and for no reason, she blasted me in response!"), conflict is a process that unfolds over time. The communication choices we make determine the course conflict takes. Everything we say and do during a conflict influences everything our partner says and does, and vice versa. Thus, the fabric of conflict is woven by our words and actions. Moreover, most conflicts proceed through several stages, each involving decisions and actions that determine the conflict's direction and consequences for the individuals involved. In its most basic form, the process of conflict involves people perceiving that a conflict exists, choosing an approach for how to handle the conflict, and then dealing with the conflict resolutions and outcomes that follow. Conflict is not a one-time-only event: how you handle a conflict with someone will have consequences for your future interactions and relationship with that person.

Finally, conflict is dynamic. Because conflict typically unfolds over a series of exchanged messages, it is ever-changing and unpredictable. Research examining the dynamic nature of conflict indicates that 66.4 percent of disputes involved conflicts that progressed via substantial shifts in topical focus (Keck & Samp, 2007). A fight over your father's snarky remark about your job transitions to a tiff over his chronic disapproval of you. Or, a dispute regarding your roommate eating your leftovers becomes an argument about relational inequity. When a conflict shifts topic, it can devolve into **kitchen-sinking** (from the expression, "throwing everything at them but the kitchen sink"), in which combatants hurl insults and accusations at each other that have little to do with the original disagreement. For example, a couple fighting over who needs to leave work early to pick up the kids may toss out accusations like: "What about the time when you completely forgot my birthday!?" and "Oh yeah?! Well, your family is weird!"

Given the intricate nature of conflict, and that often it can dynamically tangent into other troublesome topics, managing conflict is extremely challenging. We can never fully anticipate the twists and turns that may occur. But remember: *Your choices regarding your words and actions will shape everything that follows — whether tensions will escalate, the issue will resolve, or the issue will remain unresolved.* Your communication choices also influence whether your relationship with the other person (if one exists) will be damaged or grow stronger.

In our next section, we examine the approaches people use for handling conflict. But before we do, take this time to assess how you approach conflict.

SELF-QUIZ

How Do You Approach Conflict?

Read each statement. Place a check mark next to those you agree with.

During conflicts, I typically:

Avoidance

_____ keep my feelings about the disagreement to myself

_____ avoid open discussion of the dispute

_____ stay away from the topic of disagreement

_____ avoid any type of unpleasant exchange

Accommodation

_____ accommodate the other person's wishes

_____ give in to his or her desires

_____ go along with the other person's suggestions

_____ pretend to agree just to satisfy his or her expectations

Competition

_____ try to convince him or her that I'm right

_____ take control so that the decision goes in my favor

_____ pursue my side of the issue

_____ use my power to win

Reactivity

_____ explode violently with anger

_____ say things that I know will hurt him or her

_____ scream or yell loudly and throw things

_____ accuse the other person of wrongdoing

Collaboration

_____ investigate the issue of dispute to find a solution acceptable to both parties

_____ try to work with the other person to find solutions that satisfy both our expectations

_____ exchange information with him or her so we can solve the problem together

_____ bring all of our concerns out in the open so the issue can be resolved

Scoring: The category with the most check marks indicates how you primarily manage conflict. If you score equally high on two or more different approaches, you use more than one approach.

Note: Adapted from Rahim and Mager (1995); Zacchilli, Hendrick, & Hendrick (2009).

CONFLICT APPROACHES

People generally approach conflict in one of five ways: avoidance, accommodation, competition, reactivity, or collaboration (Lulofs & Cahn, 2000; Zacchilli, Hendrick, & Hendrick, 2009). Let's look at each of these in more detail.

Avoidance

One way to handle conflict is **avoidance**: ignoring the conflict, pretending it isn't really happening, or communicating indirectly about it. Avoidance is the most frequently used approach to handling conflict (Sillars, 1980). Although avoidance seems easier, less emotionally draining, and lower risk than direct confrontation (Afifi & Olson, 2005), avoidance poses substantial risks (Afifi, McManus, Steuber, & Coho, 2009). One of the biggest risks is **cumulative annoyance**, when we repress our irritations and allow them to grow as a mental list of grievances (Peterson, 2002). Eventually this list overpowers our capacities to suppress it and we suddenly explode in anger. For example, when you were a teen, your parent may have constantly reminded you to do your homework, do your chores, or even shower. This constant reminding got on your nerves, and you negated the nagging with promises of action. One evening, after a long day at school, you were again told to clean up your room. You snapped into a tirade, bellowing at your parent a list of the constant nagging instances from the last month of your life.

A second risk posed by avoidance is **pseudo-conflict**: the perception that a conflict exists when in fact it doesn't. For example, you mistakenly think your romantic partner is seeing someone else because you see tagged photos on Instagram of her arm in arm with someone else. You decide to dump your partner, despite the reality that the photos were of your partner and her cousin.

Despite these risks, choosing avoidance may be a wise option for managing conflict when emotions run high (Berscheid, 2002). If everyone involved is angry, and yet we choose to continue to engage, we run the risk of saying things that irreparably damage our relationships. Stating that you "need to cool off" before you leave, hang up, or take a break from texting may be the most adept choice.

Accommodation

Accommodation occurs when one person abandons his or her own goals to grant the desires of another person. For example, you and your siblings are buying your parents a gift for their anniversary. You have researched and carefully planned a trip; however, your siblings want to send them to a sporting event. You relinquish your idea because they are all in agreement and outnumber you.

We typically accommodate people who have more *power* than us. Why? Because if we don't, we run the risk of people exerting control or punishment over us. This highlights an important lesson regarding the relationship between power and conflict: people who are more powerful than you probably won't accommodate your goals during conflicts.

Another factor that influences people's decision to accommodate is *love*. Accommodation often reflects a high concern for others and a low concern for self; you want to please those you love (Frisby & Westerman, 2010). Thus, accommodation is likely to occur in healthy, satisfied close relationships, where selflessness is characteristic (Hendrick & Hendrick, 1992). For example, your romantic partner is accepted into a summer study-abroad program in Europe. Even though you had planned on spending the summer together, you encourage him or her to accept the offer.

Competition

Competition is when we narrowly pursue our own goals, disregarding the goals of the other. The discussion of the divergent goals is both open and clear (Sillars, 1980). Recalling that conflict begins with perception, it is not surprising that competition is motivated, in part, by negative thoughts and beliefs, including disrespect, desire to control, and a willingness to hurt others in order to gain (Bevan, Finan, & Kaminsky, 2008; Zacchilli, Hendrick, & Hendrick, 2009). Consequently, when we admire another person and care about his or her needs, we are less likely to choose competition. Conversely, if people routinely approach conflict by making demands to the exclusion of your desires, they likely do not respect you (Hendrick & Hendrick, 2006).

At a minimum, competition can trigger *defensive communication* — someone refusing to consider your goals or dismissing them as unimportant, acting superior to you, or attempting to squelch your disagreement by wielding power over you (Waldron, Turner, Alexander, & Barton, 1993). But the primary risk of choosing a competitive approach is **escalation**, a dramatic surge in the emotional intensity, negativity, or aggressiveness of the communication. When both people in conflict choose competition, and neither is willing to back down, escalation is guaranteed. Even initially trivial conflicts can quickly ignite into intense exchanges.

Reactivity

A fourth way people handle conflict is by not pursuing any conflict-related goals at all. Instead, they prioritize their own needs for expression, communicating in an emotionally explosive and negative fashion. This is known as **reactivity** and is characterized by accusations of mistrust, yelling, crying, and becoming verbally or physically abusive. Reactivity is decidedly nonstrategic. Instead of avoiding, accommodating, or competing, people simply "flip out." Similar to competition, reactivity is strongly related to a lack of respect (Bevan, Finan, & Kaminsky, 2008; Zacchilli, Hendrick, & Hendrick, 2009). People prone to reactivity have little interest in others as individuals and do not recognize others' desires as relevant (Zacchilli, Hendrick, & Hendrick, 2009).

Collaboration

The most constructive method for managing conflict is **collaboration**: treating conflict as a mutual problem-solving opportunity rather than something that must avoided, accommodated, competed over, or reacted to. Often the result of collaboration is *compromise*, when everyone involved modifies their original goals to generate a solution and resolve the conflict. We are more likely to collaborate when we respect the other person and are concerned about his or her desires, along with our own (Keck & Samp, 2007; Zacchilli, Hendrick, & Hendrick, 2009). People who regularly use collaboration feel more trust, commitment, and overall relational satisfaction compared to those who don't (Smith, Heaven, & Ciarrochi, 2008). Whenever possible, opt for collaboration.

To facilitate collaboration, try these suggestions (Wilmot & Hocker, 2001). First, *address problems rather than attack people*. Discuss the problematic topic as something separate from the people involved, such as, "This issue has really come between us." This frames the conflict around an issue rather than a person and unifies the people addressing it. At the same time, exemplify courtesy and respect, avoiding personal attacks despite how angry you may feel. This is perhaps the greatest challenge in collaboration, because you likely *will* feel angry during conflicts (Berscheid, 2002). Carefully monitor your own and others' emotions, being prepared to suggest a "time out" to allow everyone to cool down. Attempt to steer conversations back to the issue, and resist being tugged into trading insults.

Second, *focus on common interests and long-term goals rather than positions and opinions.* Resolutions sometimes arise when we rotate our perspectives. By targeting long-term goals and points of commonality, steps to a solution may surface when we pull back from our own perspectives and positions. Use inclusive "we language" (see Chapter 3) to cultivate commonality, such as, "I know we all want what's best for our company." Arguing over positions ("I want this!" versus "I want that!") endangers relationships because the conflict may devolve into a destructive contest of wills.

Third, *take the time to elicit options rather than rushing toward resolution.* Once the points of commonality and long-term goals have emerged, begin talking about resolutions by asking questions designed to elicit options: "How do you think we can best resolve this?" or "What are different ways we can solve this? Then propose ideas of your own. Be flexible and willing to negotiate a solution, rather than insisting on one. Most collaborative solutions involve some form of compromise; so be open to adapting your original desires, even if it means not getting everything you want. Then combine the best parts of the various suggestions to come up with an *agreeable* solution. Avoid fixating on a "perfect" solution — it may not exist.

Finally, *critically evaluate your solution.* Ask for everyone's assessment: "Is this equitable for all?" The pivotal point is livability: Can everyone live with the resolution in the long run? Or is it unduly biased or so short of original desires that resentments may emerge? If anyone can answer "yes" to the latter question, return to step three (above) to continue to create options until a satisfactory solution emerges for all.

The third relational challenge is providing comfort and support to others. We conclude this chapter, and our guidebook, by considering this essential issue.

EMPATHY AND SUPPORT

A third challenge we face in sustaining close interpersonal relationships is knowing how to respond to others going through hard times. Providing support is crucial for lasting closeness but is also extremely effortful. Furthermore, people's perceptions of support vary, so our best intentions may not, in fact, be seen as supportive.

Empathy is an essential skill for providing support. *Empathy* comes from the Greek word *empatheia*, meaning "feeling into." When we experience **empathy**, we "feel into" others' thoughts and emotions, attempting to understand their perspectives and discern their feelings in order to identify with them (Kuhn, 2001). But *experiencing* empathy isn't sufficient in itself to improve your interpersonal communication and relationships. You also must *convey* your empathy to others. We do so through **supportive communication** — sharing messages that express empathy and that offer personal assistance (Burleson & MacGeorge, 2002). *Competent support* sincerely expresses sympathy, condolence, and concern for others while encouraging their own emotional expression. *Incompetent support* informs others how they should feel or indicates that they are somehow inadequate or blameworthy.

Communication scholar and social support expert Amanda Holmstrom suggests seven ways we can improve our supportive communication:

1. *Make sure the person is ready to talk.* You may have amazing support skills, but if the person is too upset to talk, don't push it. Instead, make it clear that you'll be there to listen if or when he or she needs you.

2. *Find the right place and time.* Once a person *is* ready, find a place and a time conducive to quiet conversation. Avoid distracting settings, such as parties, where you won't be able to focus. Find a time of the day when neither person is pressed by obligations.

3. *Ask good questions.* Start with open-ended queries such as "How are you feeling?" or "What's on your mind?" Then gently refine your questions based on the response, such as "Are you eating and sleeping OK?" (if not, a potential indicator of depression) or "Have you connected with a support group?"

Test This One Yourself

What are some other questions you could ask? Consider three different questions you could ask, from general to specific, and try them out the next time someone needs support.

Importantly, *if you suspect a person is contemplating suicide, ask him or her directly about it.* Ask, "Have you been thinking about killing yourself?" or "Do you have a plan for suicide?" People often think that direct questions such as these will "push someone over the edge," — in fact, it's the opposite. Research suggests that someone considering suicide *wants* to talk about it but believes that no one cares. If you ask direct questions, a suicidal person typically *won't* be offended or lie but instead will open up to you. Then you will have a better idea of what the person is experiencing and can help the person get the assistance he or she needs. Someone *not* considering suicide may express surprise at the question, even laughing it off with a "What? No way!"

4. *Legitimize, don't minimize.* Don't dismiss the problem or the significance of the person's feelings by saying things such as, "It could have been worse" or "Why are you so upset!?" Research shows these comments are unhelpful. Instead, let the person know that it's normal and okay to feel what he or she is feeling. Don't assume that because you've been in a similar situation, you know what someone is going through. Refrain from saying, "I know just how you feel."

5. *Listen actively*. Show the person that you are interested in what is being said. Engage in good eye contact, lean toward him or her, and say "Uh-huh" and "Yeah" when appropriate.

6. *Offer advice cautiously*. Our instinct is to help someone who is suffering, and we may jump right to offering advice. But many times that's not helpful or even wanted. Advice is more effective when it's requested, given by someone with relevant expertise (e.g., a relationship counselor), or suggests solutions the person actually can enact. Advice is less effective when it implies that the person is incapable of solving his or her own problems or deserves blame. When in doubt, ask if advice would be appreciated — or just hold back.

7. *Show concern and give praise*. Specifically state that you sincerely care and are genuinely concerned about their well-being: "I am worried about you" or "You are really important to me." Bolster the other person by celebrating the small steps ("You slept through the night!) or praising his or her strength in handling this challenge. Showing care and concern helps connect you; sharing praise enhances the person's feelings and self-esteem.

 GAUGE YOUR KNOWLEDGE

Before finishing this chapter, refer back to the chapter-opening checklist to assess your understanding of the chapter concepts.

GLOSSARY

accommodation When one person abandons his or her own goals to grant the desires of another person.

active listeners People who set themselves apart from those who merely "listen" by doing three things when they respond: providing positive feedback, paraphrasing, and clarifying.

adaptors Touching gestures that serve a psychological or physical purpose.

algebraic impressions Carefully evaluating each new thing we learn about a person and using all available information to calculate an overall impression.

appropriateness The degree to which your communication matches situational, relational, and cultural expectations regarding how people should communicate.

assurances Messages that emphasize how much a partner means to you, emphasize how important the relationship is, and ensure a secure future together.

attending Devoting attention to received information.

attributions Creating explanations for our own and others' communication behaviors.

avoidance Ignoring the conflict, pretending it isn't really happening, or communicating indirectly about it. Avoidance is the most frequently used approach to handling conflict.

channel The sensory dimension along which communicators transmit information. Channels can be auditory (sound), visual (sight), tactile (touch), olfactory (scent), or oral (taste).

clarifying The act of asking for additional explanation regarding the person's intended meaning.

collaboration Treating conflict as a mutual problem-solving opportunity rather than something that must be avoided, accommodated, competed over, or reacted to.

commitment A strong psychological attachment to a partner and an intention to continue the relationship long into the future.

communication The process through which people use messages to generate meanings within and across contexts, cultures, channels, and media.

communication skills Repeatable goal-directed behaviors and behavioral patterns that are routinely practiced in interpersonal encounters and relationships.

competition The narrow pursuit of our own goals, with disregard to the goals of others.

conflict A process that occurs when people perceive they have incompatible goals or that someone is interfering in their ability to achieve their objectives.

context A situation that helps shape the meaning that is created by the message.

cooperative language Use of language resulting in messages that people easily can understand because they are informative, honest, relevant, and clear.

culture An established, coherent set of beliefs, attitudes, values, and practices shared by a large group of people.

cumulative annoyance The repression of our irritations that allows them to grow into a mental list of grievances.

dyadic communication Communication between two people.

effectiveness The ability to use communication to accomplish your goals.

emblems Gestures that symbolize a specific verbal meaning within a given culture, such as the "thumbs up" or the "V for victory" sign.

emotion An intense reaction to an event that involves interpreting event meaning, becoming physiologically aroused, labeling the experience as emotional, managing our reaction, and communicating through emotional displays and disclosures.

emotional intelligence (EI) The ability to interpret emotions accurately and to use this information to manage emotions, communicate them competently, and solve relationship problems.

empathy Attempting to understand others' perspectives and discern their feelings in order to identify with them.

equity The balance of rewards and costs exchanged between you and the another person.

escalation A dramatic surge in the emotional intensity, negativity, or aggressiveness of the communication.

ethics The set of moral principles that guides our behavior toward others.

family A network of people who share their lives over long periods of time and are bound by marriage, blood, or commitment; who consider themselves as family; and who share a significant history and anticipated future of functioning in a family relationship.

feelings Short-term emotional reactions to events that generate only limited arousal.

friendship A voluntary interpersonal relationship characterized by intimacy and liking.

fundamental attribution error The tendency to attribute others' behaviors solely to internal causes (the kind of person they are) rather than the social or environmental forces affecting them.

gestalt A general sense of a person that's either positive or negative, arriving at an overall judgment based on discerning a few traits.

halo effect The tendency for positive gestalts to lead us to positively interpret another's communication and behavior.

hearing Occurs when vibrations in the eardrum travel along acoustic nerves to the brain after sound waves generated from the sound source enter your inner ear.

honesty The single most important characteristic of cooperative verbal communication because other people trust that the information we share with them is truthful.

horn effect The tendency for negative gestalts to lead us to negatively interpret another's communication and behavior.

"I" language Language that emphasizes ownership of your feelings, opinions, and beliefs. For example, instead of saying "You hurt me," say "I'm feeling hurt."

illustrators Gestures that accent or mime verbal messages.

immediacy The degree to which you find someone interesting and attractive.

impersonal communication Exchanges that have a negligible perceived impact on our thoughts, emotions, behaviors, and relationships.

inequity When the benefits or contributions provided by one person are greater than those provided by the other.

informative This is sharing *enough* information, but *not* sharing *too much*.

interaction When people exchange a series of messages, whether face-to-face or through electronic devices (smart phones, tablets, etc.).

interpersonal communication A dynamic form of transactional communication between two (or more) people in which the messages exchanged significantly influence their thoughts, emotions, behaviors, and relationships.

interpersonal communication competence Consistently communicating in ways that are *appropriate* (your communication follows accepted norms), *effective* (your communication enables you to achieve your goals), and *ethical* (your communication treats people fairly).

interpersonal impressions The mental pictures we create of who people are and how we feel about them.

interpersonal relationships The emotional, mental, and physical involvements that we forge with others through our communication.

intimate space Sharing space that ranges from 0 to 18 inches, which is the distance people often occupy in close relationships.

intrapersonal communication One person talking out loud to oneself or having a mental "conversation" inside one's head.

kitchen-sinking When remarks made during a conflict shift from the original topic to an unrelated disagreement.

liking A feeling of affection and respect that we have for another person.

long-term memory The permanent information storage areas of our minds.

loving A vastly deeper and more intense emotional commitment that consists of three components: intimacy, caring, and attachment.

media Tools used for exchanging messages.

message The "package" of information that is transported through communication.

moods Low-intensity states — such as boredom, contentment, grouchiness, or serenity — that are not caused by particular events and typically last longer than feelings or emotions.

multitasking Using multiple forms of technology at once, each feeding an unrelated information stream.

nonverbal communication The intentional or unintentional transmission of meaning through an individual's *nonspoken* physical and behavioral cues.

paraphrasing Summarizing others' comments after they have finished to verify the accuracy of your understanding during both face-to-face and online encounters.

perception The process of selecting, organizing, and interpreting information from our senses.

personal space Sharing space that ranges between 18 inches and 4 feet, which is the distance people occupy during encounters with friends.

positive feedback Affirming behavior in response to a message or person, which could include looking directly at the person speaking, smiling, positioning your body to face the speaker, and leaning forward.

positivity Communicating in a cheerful, sunny, and optimistic fashion; doing unsolicited favors; and giving unexpected gifts.

proportional justice The balance between benefits gained from the relationship versus contributions made to the relationship.

pseudo-conflict The perception that a conflict exists when in fact it doesn't.

public space The distance between people ranging upward from 12 feet, including great distances; this span occurs most often during formal occasions such as public speeches or college lectures.

reactivity Communicating in an emotionally explosive and negative fashion.

recalling The act of remembering information after you've received, attended to, understood, and responded to it.

receiving Processing a message.

regulators Gestures that control the exchange of conversational turns during interpersonal encounters, such as when you point a finger while trying to interrupt or hold your palm straight up to keep a person from interrupting.

relational dialectics Competing tensions between ourselves and our feelings toward others in close relationships.

relational maintenance Using communication and supportive behaviors to sustain a desired relationship status and level of satisfaction.

relevance Making your conversational contributions responsive to what others have said.

romantic relationship A chosen interpersonal involvement forged through communication in which the participants perceive the bond as romantic.

seeing When optic nerves become stimulated and send information to your brain, which translates the information into visual images.

self-awareness The ability to step outside yourself (so to speak); see yourself as a unique person distinct from your surroundings; and reflect on your thoughts, feelings, and behaviors.

self-concept The overall perception of one's self.

self-disclosure When people share their "inner" selves with others, revealing personal, private information.

self-esteem The overall evaluation that you assign to your self-concept.

self-fulfilling prophecies Predictions about future outcomes that lead us to behave in ways that generate those outcomes.

sharing tasks Taking mutual responsibility for practical demands that arise in our lives and negotiating an equitable division of labor.

short-term memory To temporarily house information as we make sense of its meaning.

social exchange theory The idea that we forge and continue relationships with those we see offering substantial rewards (resources we like and want) with few associated costs (things demanded of us in return).

social space Sharing space that ranges from about 4 to 12 feet. Many people use it when communicating in the workplace or with acquaintances and strangers.

supportive communication Sharing messages that express empathy and that offer personal assistance.

understanding Interpreting the meaning of another's communication by comparing newly received information against past knowledge.

verbal communication Exchanges of spoken or written language with others during interactions.

"you" language The use of language to focus attention and blame on other people, such as "*You* let us down."

REFERENCES

Afifi, T. D. (2003). "Feeling caught" in stepfamilies: Managing boundary turbulence through appropriate communication privacy rules. *Journal of Social and Personal Relationships, 20*(6), 729–755.

Afifi, T. D., McManus, T., Steuber, K., & Coho, A. (2009). Verbal avoidance and dissatisfaction in intimate conflict situations. *Human Communication Research, 35,* 357–383.

Afifi, T. D., & Olson, L. (2005). The chilling effect and the pressure to conceal secrets in families. *Communication Monographs, 72,* 192–216.

Anderson, N. H. (1981). *Foundations of information integration theory.* Orlando, FL: Academic Press.

Arriaga, X. B., & Agnew, C. R. (2001). Being committed: Affective, cognitive, and conative components of relationship commitment. *Personality and Social Psychology Bulletin, 27,* 1190–1203.

Asch, S. E. (1946). Forming impressions of personality. *Journal of Abnormal and Social Psychology, 41,* 258–290.

Barker, L. L. (1971). *Listening behavior.* Englewood Cliffs, NJ: Prentice Hall.

Baxter, L. A. (1990). Dialectical contradictions in relationship development. *Journal of Social and Personal Relationships, 7,* 69–88.

Benoit, P. J., & Benoit, W. E. (1990). To argue or not to argue. In R. Trapp & J. Schuetz (Eds.), *Perspectives on argumentation: Essays in honor of Wayne Brockriede* (pp. 55–72). Prospect Heights, IL: Waveland Press.

Berscheid, E. (2002). Emotion. In H. H. Kelley et al. (Eds.), *Close relationships* (2nd ed., pp. 110–168). Clinton Corners, NY: Percheron Press.

Berscheid, E., & Regan, P. (2005). *The psychology of interpersonal relationships.* Upper Saddle River, NJ: Pearson Education.

Bevan, J. L., Finan, A., & Kaminsky, A. (2008). Modeling serial arguments in close relationships: The serial argument process model. *Human Communication Research, 34,* 600–624.

Braithwaite, D. O., Bach, B. W., Baxter, L. A., DiVerniero, R., Hammonds, J. R., Hosek, A. M., et al. (2010). Constructing family: A typology of voluntary kin. *Journal of Social and Personal Relationships, 27*(3), 388–407. doi: 10.1177/0265407510361615

Brehm, S. S., Miller, R. S., Perlman, D., & Campbell, S. M. (2002). *Intimate relationships* (3rd ed.). Boston, MA: McGraw-Hill.

Brend, R. (1975). Male–female intonation patterns in American English. In B. Thorne & N. Henley (Eds.), *Language and sex: Difference and dominance* (pp. 84–87). Rowley, MA: Newbury House.

Bunkers, S. S. (2010). The power and possibility in listening. *Nursing Science Quarterly, 23*(1), 22–27.

Burgoon, M. (1995). A kinder, gentler discipline: Feeling good about being mediocre. In B. R. Burleson (Ed.), *Communication yearbook 18* (pp. 464–479). Thousand Oaks, CA: Sage.

Burleson, B. R., & MacGeorge, E. L. (2002). Supportive communication. In M. L. Knapp & J. A. Daly (Eds.), *Handbook of interpersonal communication* (pp. 374–422). Thousand Oaks, CA: Sage.

Cacioppo, J. T., Klein, D. J., Berntson, G. G., & Hatfield, E. (1993). The psychophysiology of emotion. In M. Lewis & J. M. Haviland (Eds.), *Handbook of emotions* (pp. 119–142). New York, NY: Guilford Press.

Canary, D. J. (2003). Managing interpersonal conflict: A model of events related to strategic choices. In J. O. Greene & B. R. Burleson (Eds.), *Handbook of communication and social interaction skills.* Mahwah, NJ: Erlbaum.

Canary, D. J., Emmers-Sommer, T. M., & Faulkner, S. (1997). *Sex and gender differences in personal relationships.* New York, NY: Guilford Press.

Carducci, B. J., & Zimbardo, P. G. (1995, November/December). Are you shy? *Psychology Today, 28,* 34–41.

Carr, N. (2010). *The shallows: What the Internet is doing to our brains.* New York, NY: W. W. Norton.

Crosnoe, R., & Cavanagh, S. E. (2010). Families with children and adolescents: A review, critique, and future agenda. *Journal of Marriage and Family, 72,* 594–611.

Dainton, M., & Stafford, L. (1993). Routine maintenance behaviors: A comparison of relationship type, partner similarity and sex differences. *Journal of Social and Personal Relationships, 10,* 255–271.

Daly, J. (1975). *Listening and interpersonal evaluations.* Paper presented at the annual meeting of the Central States Speech Association, Kansas City, MO.

Davis, K. E., & Todd, M. L. (1985). Assessing friendship: Prototypes, paradigm cases, and relationship description. In S. Duck & D. Perlman (Eds.), *Understanding personal relationships: An interdisciplinary approach* (pp. 17–38). London, UK: Sage.

Dindia, K., & Allen, M. (1992). Sex differences in self-disclosure: A meta-analysis. *Psychological Bulletin, 112,* 106–124.

Ekman, P., & Friesen, W. V. (1969). The repertoire of nonverbal behavior: Categories, origins, usage, and coding. *Semiotica, 1,* 49–98.

Englehardt, E. E. (2001). Introduction to ethics in interpersonal communication. In E. E. Englehardt (Ed.), *Ethical issues in interpersonal communication: Friends, intimates, sexuality, marriage, and family* (pp. 1–27). Orlando, FL: Harcourt College.

Environmental Protection Agency. (2002, September). Cross-cultural communication. Retrieved from http://www.epa.gov/superfund/communicatiy/pdfs/12ccc.pdf

Frijda, N. H. (2005). Emotion experience. *Cognition and Emotion, 19,* 473–497.

Frisby, B. N., & Westerman, D. (2010). Rational actors: Channel selection and rational choices in romantic conflict episodes. *Journal of Social and Personal Relationships, 27,* 970–981.

Galvin, K. M., Brommel, B. J., & Bylund, C. L. (2004). *Family communication: Cohesion and change* (6th ed.). New York, NY: Pearson.

Glenn, D. (2010, February 28). Divided attention: In an age of classroom multitasking, scholars probe the nature of learning and memory. *The Chronicle of Higher Education.* Retrieved from http://chronicle.com/article/Scholars-Turn-Their-Attention/63746/

Golish, T. D. (2000). Changes in closeness between adult children and their parents: A turning point analysis. *Communication Reports, 13,* 79–97.

Golish, T. D. (2003). Stepfamily communication strengths: Understanding the ties that bind. *Human Communication Research, 29*(1), 41–80.

Grice, H. P. (1989). *Studies in the way of words.* Cambridge, MA: Harvard University Press.

Gross, J. J., & John, O. P. (2002). Wise emotion regulation. In L. Feldman Barrett & P. Salovey (Eds.), *The wisdom in feeling: Psychological processes in emotional intelligence* (pp. 297–319). New York, NY: Guilford Press.

Gross, J. J., Richards, J. M., & John, O. P. (2006). Emotion regulation in everyday life. In D. K. Snyder, J. A. Simpson, & J. N. Hughes (Eds.), *Emotion regulation in couples and families: Pathways to dysfunction and health.* Washington, DC: American Psychological Association.

Gudykunst, W. B., & Kim, Y. Y. (2003). *Communicating with strangers: An approach to intercultural communication* (4th ed.). New York, NY: McGraw-Hill.

Haas, S. M., & Stafford, L. (2005). Maintenance behaviors in same-sex and marital relationships: A matched sample comparison. *Journal of Family Communication, 5,* 43–60.

Hall, E. T. (1966). A system of the notation of proxemics behavior. *American Anthropologist, 65,* 1003–1026.

Hatfield, E. (1983). Equity theory and research: An overview. In H. H. Blumberg, A. P. Hare, V. Kent, & M. Davies (Eds.), *Small groups and social interaction* (Vol. 2, pp. 401–412). Chichester, UK: Wiley.

Heider, F. (1958). *The psychology of interpersonal relations.* New York, NY: Wiley.

Hendrick, S. S., & Hendrick, C. (1992). *Romantic love.* Thousand Oaks, CA: Sage.

Hendrick, S. S., & Hendrick, C. (2006). Measuring respect in close relationships. *Journal of Social and Personal Relationships, 23,* 881–899.

Hodgson, L. K., & Wertheim, E. H. (2007). Does good emotion management aid forgiving? Multiple dimensions of empathy, emotion management and forgiving of self and others. *Journal of Social and Personal Relationships, 24*(6), 931–949.

Jacobs, S., Dawson, E. J., & Brashers, D. (1996). Information manipulation theory: A replication and assessment. *Communication Monographs, 63,* 70–82.

Johnson, A. J., Wittenberg, E., Villagran, M. M., Mazur, M., & Villagran, P. (2003). Relational progression as a dialectic: Examining turning points in communication among friends. *Communication Monographs, 70*(3), 230–249.

Joinson, A. N. (2001, March/April). Self-disclosure in computer-mediated communication: The role of self-awareness and visual anonymity. *European Journal of Social Psychology, 31,* 177–192.

Jourard, S. M. (1964). *The transparent self.* New York, NY: Van Nostrand Reinhold.

Kahneman, D. (1973). *Attention and effort.* Englewood Cliffs, NJ: Prentice Hall.

Keck, K. L., & Samp, J. A. (2007). The dynamic nature of goals and message production as revealed in a sequential analysis of conflict interactions. *Human Communication Research, 33,* 27–47.

Keesing, R. M. (1974). Theories of culture. *Annual Review of Anthropology, 3,* 73–97.

Kelley, H. H., & Thibaut, J. W. (1978). *Interpersonal relations: A theory of interdependence.* New York, NY: Wiley.

Klopf, D. W. (2001). *Intercultural encounters: The fundamentals of intercultural communication* (5th ed.). Englewood, CO: Morton.

Knapp, M. L., & Hall, J. A. (2002). *Nonverbal communication in human interaction* (5th ed.). Belmont, CA: Wadsworth/Thomson Learning.

Koerner, A. F., & Fitzpatrick, M. A. (2006). Family communication patterns theory: A social cognitive approach. In D. O. Braithwaite & L. A. Baxter (Eds.), *Engaging theories in family communication: Multiple perspectives* (pp. 50–65). Thousand Oaks, CA: Sage.

Kotzé, M., & Venter, I. (2011). Differences in emotional intelligence between effective and ineffective leaders in the public sector: An empirical study. *International Review of Administrative Sciences, 77*(2), 397–427.

Krause, J. (2001). *Properties of naturally produced clear speech at normal rates and implications for intelligibility enhancement* (Unpublished doctoral dissertation). Massachusetts Institute of Technology, Cambridge, MA.

Kubany, E. S., Richard, D. C., Bauer, G. B., & Muraoka, M. Y. (1992). Impact of assertive and accusatory communication of distress and anger: A verbal component analysis. *Aggressive Behavior, 18,* 337–347.

Kuhn, J. L. (2001). Toward an ecological humanistic psychology. *Journal of Humanistic Psychology, 41,* 9–24.

Kurdek, L. A. (2005). What do we know about gay and lesbian couples? *Current Directions in Psychological Science, 14,* 251–254.

Le, B., Korn, M. S., Crockett, E. E., & Loving, T. J. (2010). Missing you maintains us: Missing a romantic partner, commitment, relationship maintenance, and physical infidelity. *Journal of Social and Personal Relationships, 28,* 653–667.

Lulofs, R. S., & Cahn, D. D. (2000). *Conflict: From theory to action* (2nd ed.). Needham Heights, MA: Allyn & Bacon.

Macrae, C. N., & Bodenhausen, G. V. (2001). Social cognition: Categorical person perception. *British Journal of Psychology, 92,* 239–255.

Malis, R. S., & Roloff, M. E. (2006). Demand/withdraw patterns in serial arguments: Implications for well-being. *Human Communication Research, 32,* 198–216.

Mashek, D. J., & Aron, A. (2004). *Handbook of closeness and intimacy.* Mahwah, NJ: Erlbaum.

Mauss, I. B., Levenson, R. W., McCarter, L., Wilhelm, F. H., & Gross, J. J. (2005). The tie that binds: Coherence among emotion experience, behavior, and physiology. *Emotion, 5,* 175–190.

Mayer, J. D., Salovey, P., & Caruso, D. R. (2004). Emotional intelligence: Theory, findings and implications. *Psychological Inquiry, 15*(3), 197–215.

McCornack, S. A. (2008). Information manipulation theory: Explaining how deception works. In L. A. Baxter & D. O. Braithwaite (Eds.), *Engaging theories in interpersonal communication: Multiple perspectives* (pp. 215–226). Thousand Oaks, CA: Sage.

McEwan, B., Babin Gallagher, B., & Farinelli, L. (2008, November). *The end of a friendship: Friendship dissolution reasons and methods.* Paper presented at the annual meeting of the National Communication Association, San Diego, CA.

McNaughton, D., Hamlin, D., McCarthy, J., Head-Reeves, D., & Schreiner, M. (2007). Learning to listen: Teaching an active listening strategy to preservice education professionals. *Topics in Early Childhood Special Education, 27*(4), 223–231.

Mehrabian, A. (1972). *Nonverbal communication.* Chicago, IL: Aldine.

Metts, S., & Planalp, S. (2002). Emotional communication. In M. L. Knapp & J. A. Daly (Eds.), *Handbook of interpersonal communication* (pp. 339–373). Thousand Oaks, CA: Sage.

Miller, G. R., & Steinberg, M. (1975). *Between people: A new analysis of interpersonal communication.* Chicago, IL: Science Research Associates.

Miller, L., Hefner, V., & Scott, A. (2007, May). *Turning points in dyadic friendship development and termination.* Paper presented at the annual meeting of the International Communication Association, San Francisco, CA.

Miller, R. S., Perlman, D., & Brehm, S. S. (2007). Love: Chapter 8. In R. S. Miller, D. Perlman, & S. S. Brehm (Eds.), *Intimate relationships* (pp. 244–275). New York, NY: McGraw-Hill.

Montagu, M. F. A. (1971). *Touching: The human significance of the skin.* New York, NY: Columbia University Press.

Myers, D. G. (2002). *The pursuit of happiness: Discovering the pathway to fulfillment, well-being, and enduring personal joy.* New York, NY: HarperCollins.

National Communication Association (NCA). (2002, October). *The field of communication.* Retrieved from http://www.natcom.org/Tertiary.aspx?id=236

Ophir, E., Nass, C. I., & Wagner, A. D. (2012). Cognitive control in media multitaskers. *Proceedings of the National Academy of Sciences.* Retrieved from http://www.pnas.org/content/106/37/15583

Parkinson, B., Totterdell, P., Briner, R. B., & Reynolds, S. (1996). *Changing moods: The psychology of mood and mood regulation.* London, UK: Longman.

Parks, M. R. (1994). Communicative competence and interpersonal control. In M. L. Knapp & G. R. Miller (Eds.), *Handbook of interpersonal communication* (2nd ed., pp. 589–620). Beverly Hills, CA: Sage.

Parks, M. R., & Floyd, K. (1996). Making friends in cyberspace. *Journal of Communication, 46,* 80–97.

Patterson, B. R. (2007). Relationship development revisited: A preliminary look at communication in friendship over the lifespan. *Communication Research Reports, 24*(1), 29–37.

Patterson, M. L. (1995). A parallel process model of nonverbal communication. *Journal of Nonverbal Behavior, 19,* 3–29.

Pennebaker, J. W. (1997). *Opening up: The healing power of expressing emotions.* New York, NY: Guilford Press.

Peterson, D. R. (2002). Conflict. In H. H. Kelley et al. (Eds.), *Close relationships* (2nd ed., pp. 360–396). Clinton Corners, NY: Percheron Press.

Rabby, M. K. (1997, November). *Maintaining relationships via electronic mail.* Paper presented at the annual meeting of the National Communication Association, Chicago, IL.

Rahim, M. A., & Mager, N. R. (1995). Confirmatory factor analysis of the styles of handling interpersonal conflict: First-order factor model and its invariance across groups. *Journal of Applied Psychology, 80,* 122–132.

Rawlins, W. K. (1992). *Friendship matters: Communication, dialectics, and the life course.* New York, NY: Aldine de Gruyter.

Reis, H. T., & Patrick, B. C. (1996). Attachment and intimacy: Component processes. In E. T. Higgins & A. W. Kruglanski (Eds.), *Social psychology: Handbook of basic principles* (pp. 523–563). New York, NY: Guilford Press.

Reis, H. T., & Shaver, P. (1988). Intimacy as an interpersonal process. In S. W. Duck (Ed.), *Handbook of personal relationships* (pp. 367–389). New York, NY: Wiley.

Roloff, M. E., & Soule, K. P. (2002). Interpersonal conflict: A review. In M. L. Knapp & J. A. Daly (Eds.), *Handbook of interpersonal communication* (3rd ed., pp. 475–528). Thousand Oaks, CA: Sage.

Rosenfeld, H. M. (1987). Conversational control functions of nonverbal behavior. In A. W. Siegman & S. Feldstein (Eds.), *Nonverbal behavior and communication* (2nd ed., pp. 563–602). Hillsdale, NJ: Erlbaum.

Rubin, L. B. (1996). Reflections on friendship. In K. M. Galvin & P. J. Cooper (Eds.), *Making connections: Readings in relational communication* (pp. 254–257). Los Angeles, CA: Roxbury.

Rubin, Z. (1973). *Liking and loving: An invitation to social psychology.* New York, NY: Holt, Rinehart & Winston.

Rusbult, C. E., Arriaga, X. B., & Agnew, C. R. (2001). Interdependence in close relationships. In G. J. O. Fletcher & M. S. Clark (Eds.), *Blackwell handbook of social psychology, vol. 2: Interpersonal processes* (pp. 359–387*).* Oxford: Blackwell.

Shelton, J. N., Trail, T. E., West, T. V., & Bergsieker, H. B. (2010). From strangers to friends: The interpersonal process model of intimacy in developing interracial friendships. *Journal of Social and Personal Relationships, 27*(1), 71–90.

Sias, P. M., Drzewiecka, J. A., Meares, M., Bent, R., Konomi, Y., Ortega, M., & White, C. (2008). Intercultural friendship development. *Communication Reports, 21*(1), 1–13.

Sillars, A. L. (1980). Attributions and communication in roommate conflicts. *Communication Monographs, 47*, 180–200.

Sillars, A., Smith, T., & Koerner, A. (2010). Misattributions contributing to empathic (in)accuracy during parent–adolescent conflict discussions. *Journal of Social and Personal Relationships, 27*(6), 727–747.

Silverstein, M., & Giarrusso, R. (2010). Aging and family life: A decade review. *Journal of Marriage and Family, 72*, 1039–1058.

Smith, L., Heaven, P. C. L., & Ciarrochi, J. (2008). Trait emotional intelligence, conflict communication patterns, and relationship satisfaction. *Personality and Individual Differences, 44*, 1314–1325.

Spender, D. (1990). *Man made language*. London: Pandora Press.

Spitzberg, B. (1997). A model of intercultural communication competence. In L. A. Samovar & R. E. Porter (Eds.), *Intercultural communication: A reader* (pp. 379–391). Belmont, CA: Wadsworth.

Spitzberg, B. H., & Cupach, W. R. (1984). *Interpersonal communication competence*. Beverly Hills, CA: Sage.

Spitzberg, B. H., & Cupach, W. R. (2002). Interpersonal skills. In M. L. Knapp & J. A. Daly (Eds.), *Handbook of interpersonal communication* (3rd ed., pp. 564–611). Thousand Oaks, CA: Sage.

Sprecher, S. (2001). A comparison of emotional consequences of and changes in equity over time using global and domain-specific measures of equity. *Journal of Social and Personal Relationships, 18*, 477–501.

Stafford, L. (2003). Maintaining romantic relationships: A summary and analysis of one research program. In D. J. Canary & M. Dainton (Eds.), *Maintaining relationships through communication: Relational, contextual, and cultural variations* (pp. 51–77). Mahwah, NJ: Erlbaum.

Stafford, L. (2010). Measuring relationship maintenance behaviors: Critique and development of the revised relationship maintenance behavior scale. *Journal of Social and Personal Relationships, 28*, 278–303.

Stafford, L., Dainton, M., & Haas, S. (2000). Measuring routine and strategic relational maintenance: Scale revision, sex versus gender roles, and the prediction of relational characteristics. *Communication Monographs, 67*, 306–323.

Strauss, V. (2006, March 21). Putting parents in their place: Outside class. *The Washington Post*, p. A08.

Streek, J. (1993). Gesture as communication I: Its coordination with gaze and speech. *Communication Monographs, 60*, 275–299.

Tardy, C. H. (2000). Self-disclosure and health: Revising Sidney Jourard's hypothesis. In S. Petronio (Ed.), *Balancing the secrets of private disclosures* (pp. 111–122). Mahwah, NJ: Erlbaum.

Tardy, C., & Dindia, K. (1997). Self-disclosure. In O. Hargie (Ed.), *The handbook of communication skills*. London, UK: Routledge.

Tovares, A. V. (2010). All in the family: Small stories and narrative construction of a shared family identity that includes pets. *Narrative Inquiry, 20*(1), 1–19.

Waldron, H. B., Turner, C. W., Alexander, J. F., & Barton, C. (1993). Coding defensive and supportive communications: Discriminant validity and subcategory convergence. *Journal of Family Psychology, 7*, 197–203.

Warr, P. B., & Payne, R. (1982). Experiences of strain and pleasure among British adults. *Social Science & Medicine, 16*(19), 1691–1697.

Watzlawick, P., Beavin, J. H., & Jackson, D. D. (1967). *Pragmatics of human communication: A study of interactional patterns, pathologies, and paradoxes*. New York, NY: Norton.

Wheeless, L. R. (1978). A follow-up study of the relationships among trust, disclosure, and interpersonal solidarity. *Human Communication Research, 4*, 143–145.

Wiemann, J. M. (1977). Explication and test of a model of communicative competence. *Human Communication Research, 3*, 195–213.

Wilmot, W. W., & Hocker, J. L. (2010). *Interpersonal conflict* (8th ed.). Boston, MA: McGraw-Hill.

Wolvin, A., & Coakley, C. G. (1996). *Listening*. Madison, WI: Brown & Benchmark.

Zacchilli, T. L., Hendrick, C., & Hendrick, S. S. (2009). The romantic partner conflict scale: A new scale to measure relationship conflict. *Journal of Social and Personal Relationships, 26*, 1073–1096.